The Legacy of Bear Mountain
V O L U M E   2

The Legacy of Bear Mountain

VOLUME 2

More Stories of Old Mountain Values
That Enrich Our Lives Today

Janie Mae Jones McKinley

Charleston, SC
www.PalmettoPublishing.com

The Legacy of Bear Mountain, Volume 2

First Edition: December 2020

Paperback ISBN: 978-1-64990-938-1

See the website: *www.legacyofbearmountain.com*

The cover design shows Granny and Grandpa's 1895 home on Bear Mountain. The original oil painting, now displayed at the Mountain Heritage Center Museum on the campus of Western Carolina University, was created by the late Mrs. Myrtle Pace. This talented folk artist was also a native of Zirconia, NC. Since there had never been a photograph made of the house, Mrs. Pace worked from Janie Mae's crayon drawing to recreate the beauty of the Bear Mountain home place.

Thanks to Ms. Jennifer Heaslip, Managing Editor at the *Times-News*, and her staff for their dedication, effort, and encouragement to include these local stories in the newspaper. Through these columns I have received a lot of feedback from Henderson County natives like myself whose own grandmas lived much the way Granny did. Even newcomers to our area have said they can relate to old-time stories since many of their grandparents lived on one-family farms. Since I have no heirs, writing these regular short stories has kept me even more motivated to leave a record of the old ways BACK IN THE DAY, and for this I am grateful.

Contents

List of Photos

Preface

These are stories from Back in the Day, both figuratively and literally. They comprise over three years of regular columns in the Hendersonville, North Carolina *Times-News*, some new stories, and a couple of centuries of local history.

Janie Mae Jones McKinley is a Henderson County native who lived many of these narratives, and vividly recalls her life with Granny and Grandpa on Bear Mountain. In remarkable detail, she describes a local farm so secluded that a road and electricity would not become available until 1975, decades after Grandpa's death. Accessed by a stagecoach trail, the Bear Mountain farmhouse had been built in 1895. Featuring real glass windows and doors inside the house as well as outside, the house was considered to be quite modern at the time.

Some newspaper columns elaborate on themes and stories Janie Mae included in a previous book, *The Legacy of Bear Mountain*. Others compare Granny's life with modern times and discuss the effects of the 2020 Coronavirus.

Each article is designed to be freestanding with enough information to introduce a new reader to the olden days on Bear Mountain. A specific column will focus on one small aspect of a day in Granny's life when she baked a cake, pieced a quilt, or carried water from the spring. When these stories are grouped together in a book, some of them may seem to overlap. Taken as a whole, they show perseverance, creativity, and a spirit of gratefulness for a good life on a secluded farm. Instead of focusing on the inconveniences of using oil lamps or cutting wood for the cookstove, Granny's favorite saying was, "We live right well on the mountain."

Janie Mae invites you to explore your own family legacy as you revisit the old days with her grandparents. Their gratefulness for what they considered to be a good life on their farm is thought-provoking in our modern times. Stories from so long ago may remind you of your grandparents' lives, as well.

In addition to these past articles, you are invited to read an ongoing monthly *BACK IN THE DAY* column included in the Sunday *Blue Ridge Living* section of the *Times-News*. Articles are accessible in both the print and online editions.

The *Times-News* has made a diligent effort to preserve and share local history through these columns, and Janie Mae enjoys being a part of their interest in and dedication to Henderson County. Janie Mae invites you to explore your own family legacy as you revisit the old days with her grandparents. Their gratefulness for what they considered to be a good life on their farm is thought-provoking in our modern times.

In addition to these past articles, you are invited to read an ongoing monthly *BACK IN THE DAY* column included in the Sunday *Blue Ridge Living* section of the *Times-News*. Articles are accessible in both the print and online editions.

The *Times-News* has made a diligent effort to preserve and share local history through these columns, and Janie Mae enjoys being a part of their interest in and dedication to Henderson County.

The Legacy of Bear Mountain

*Stories of Old Mountain Values
That Enrich Our Lives Today*

Janie Mae Jones McKinley

The Legacy of Bear Mountain is a previous book. It has more stories and further describes Granny and Grandpa's good life on Bear Mountain. Books by Janie Mae are available at the following places:

Historic Court House Gift Shop in Hendersonville, NC
Hendersonville Genealogical and Historical Society
Hendersonville Curb Market
M.A. Pace General Store in Saluda, NC
Amazon.com

PACKING SLIP
Larry and Janie Mae McKinley
April 14, 2021

The Legacy of Bear Mountain, Volume 2 –
OUR GIFT TO YOU

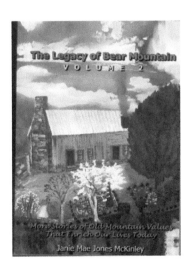

Winter Stories

1. *Winter snows still cover the old home place on Bear Mountain.*

During the Great Depression, Granny shared with kinfolks at Christmas

I n the weeks before Christmas during the 1930s, Granny often worried and thought about her extended family. She knew some of them wouldn't have a good Christmas, and she brooded over their circumstances.

The financial effects of the economic slump were real, and inadequate income over long periods of time lowered expectations. During hard times, mountain people weren't anticipating gifts, and some weren't expecting to have extra foods, either.

So, Granny's idea of a big Christmas was a holiday dinner. She knew some of her own relatives wouldn't have such a special meal, so she spent hours planning ways to share. Modern people would think life on Bear Mountain was so tough that Granny shouldn't have bothered about "pore kinfolks" or anybody else, either.

And some Christmases were harder, depending on how long Grandpa might have been out of work that year. Because of a national unemployment rate of 25 percent, benefits for laid-off workers were gradually being legislated in Washington, D.C.

But for most of the 1930s, Grandpa was paid only for the days Southern Railway needed crossties replaced. Like other companies, the railroad sometimes found it necessary to reduce expenses during the Great Depression.

This reality required Granny to plan ahead for a festive dinner, though she still had more options than some folks. When there was work for local trackmen, Grandpa earned approximately 35 cents per hour.

Back then, the cost of large bags of flour and sugar averaged about five cents a pound. So, with careful management, Granny could have extra supplies, including flavorings and spices, on hand. The first week of December she also started saving eggs. She wanted to have enough for seasonal baking since chickens laid fewer eggs during cold weather.

Along with vegetables, milk, and butter from the farm, she could usually manage to assemble the ingredients for a good dinner. Her wintertime, company menu included chicken and dumplings, cornbread and biscuits, home-canned green beans and corn, pickled peaches, and pickled beets. Sweet potatoes, stored in the can house, were ready to be baked, and a skillet of fried cabbage was always a favorite. Granny preserved late-summer cabbages upside-down in the field, so they stayed fresh.

After the meal, she served homemade desserts with cups of steaming coffee. At about 30 cents per pound in those days, coffee was considered to be an extravagance. But it "shore was tasty" with Granny's eight-layer, pumpkin pies. They were special and unique, like her memorable walnut cakes. Over the years, Granny creatively developed her own recipes using what they grew on the farm.

With the annual pumpkin harvest in the fall, she also gathered mountain walnuts. Then, she dried the nuts in the woodshed for several weeks. With sharp, hammer blows, she carefully cracked them on a huge rock in the yard. But on freezing days Granny carried buckets of shattered shells inside by the fire to finish removing the walnut pieces. That was a practical solution since it took a full morning to crack out a pound of walnut fragments.

The mellow flavor of her cake came from walnut meal mixed into the batter and icing. Food processors hadn't been invented, and there was no electricity on Bear Mountain anyway. So, Granny thought of an ingenious way to make walnut meal. She sewed a denim sack, filled it with nutmeats, and beat the sack with a hammer. In a few minutes, she had finely ground meal.

Baking nutmeal in the cake layers made them rich and dense. While they cooled, she made 7-Minute Icing (which is aptly named). Using a hand-operated eggbeater, Granny whipped the icing continuously for seven minutes while it cooked on the woodstove.

Stirring walnut meal into the icing turned it a caramel color that looked scrumptious as she frosted the layers. For extra richness and decoration, she artfully overlaid the finished cake with the prettiest walnut halves she had reserved. Now, she was ready to serve Christmas dinner.

Two stories of Granny's Depression-era generosity have been passed down through the family.

During those years, her elderly parents lived on a small farm several miles away. Her father's finances had never been stable, and in recent times, her mother had returned from a lengthy hospitalization. Although she seemed to be recovering, their funds were seriously depleted.

2. *Granny's parents: Joshua Burrell (1858 - 1938) and Hulda Jane Jones Burrell (1868 - 1960). Notice her floor-length dress and the building with hand-hewn wooden shingles in the mountainous background. This Jones family photo was artistically hand-tinted by Miss Virgie Jane Russell during the late 1930s.*

Prospects for Christmas were slim, and Granny thought and pondered how she could help. Then, she came up with a plan. Her brother lived about a mile away, and he had a logging truck with which he earned his living.

There were no roads to Bear Mountain, so Granny walked the trail to his house to share her proposal: If he could take his truck to their parents' home on Christmas Eve, he could bring them to his house. Then, they could walk to Granny's, stay overnight, and spend Christmas Day with her.

Her brother obligingly said he wouldn't have thought of the idea himself but was glad she did; he had been concerned about their parents, too.

Excitedly, Granny returned home and began preparing and baking. Watching through the kitchen window that December afternoon, she was thrilled to see "Ma and Pa" coming up the path beside the garden fence. She cooked them a delicious supper and breakfast, even before her main meal was ready.

Granny so enjoyed their overnight visit, and they appreciated her holiday invitation. Then, she and Grandpa helped carry "pasteboard" boxes of special foods to load onto the logging truck when they returned home. Granny treasured that Christmas because her father passed away not long afterward.

The other account of Granny's thoughtfulness was when her brother and his family experienced a lot of sickness and loss of income. They had several small children who weren't expecting much from Santa's visit.

Granny suggested that she prepare Christmas dinner so their limited resources could be stretched further. Again, she planned and cooked a meal featuring her special desserts. With the help of her daughter, who was working at the Zirconia Post Office by that time, they provided a tree and small presents for the children, too.

In a rural Post Office, the Postmaster and his employees were paid more in "local status" than in actual money. In the late 1930s, the government stipend for the Postal Clerk's position was $3.00 per week. But it bought a lot, and years later I heard the story about trimming a table-top, Christmas tree.

Icicles were probably the least-expensive decoration at F.W. Woolworth's 5 & 10 Cent Store on Hendersonville's Main Street. The box contained hundreds of flimsy, silver-foil strips (that oftentimes matted together). Each slivered piece was over a foot long, and Granny patiently untangled and hung them—one at a time.

Even without electricity, the little pine tree from the Bear Mountain forest was beautifully transformed. At night, it gleamed and sparkled in the kerosene lamplight. And, to everyone's delight, the decorated tree shimmered in the slightest breeze when the living-room door was opened during the day.

With foil icicles, dime-store gifts, and her seasonal dinner, Granny shared what was available during the Great Depression. And her caring efforts helped to make Christmas merrier during hard times.

You can probably recall similar kindnesses, concern, and sharing in your family. Perhaps simple decorations were displayed on trees cut from the forest; farm-based, holiday dinners and small gifts might have been enjoyed back then, as well.

Be sure to retell those stories this year, so the events and traditions of long-ago Christmases will be remembered—and passed on to younger generations.

Countryfolks sold Christmas greenery on Main Street

Hendersonville once had thriving Christmas-greenery businesses on Main Street. In the late 1940s, downtown was especially lively in December. It was the only place to shop before shopping centers and the development of Four Seasons Boulevard.

The popularity of artificial Christmas trees was still decades into the future. So, just after World War II, fresh Christmas trees were in great demand. People wanted pine fragrance in the house and a hemlock wreath on the door.

Countryfolks had mountainsides of greenery to sell to townspeople who couldn't grow their own. These seasonal street vendors developed loyal customers in Hendersonville who returned every year.

Just after Thanksgiving, pick-up trucks began arriving to claim prime parking spots at various intersections. The corners of Main Street at 4th Avenue (near the big clock at the bank) were considered the best locations.

Creative country ladies had been busy handcrafting dozens of wreaths from the graceful limbs of fresh hemlock. Mountain holly, heavy with red berries, along with pine cones gathered from the forest, added finishing touches.

3. Mr. Roland Hoots (1940-2021) of the Carolina Mountain Car Club with his 1936 Ford pickup during the years Mr. Cliff Mullinax, Jr., operated a Christmas tree business on South Main Street.

Proudly displayed on wooden sideboards of pick-up trucks, these beautifully designed creations enhanced the holiday decor of Hendersonville's bustling Main Street. White pine and cedar Christmas trees, harvested daily, leaned along the sides of the trucks. Holly branches, turkey paw (ground pine), boxwood and pine boughs, displayed on truck hoods, waited to decorate special mantles.

Mountain mistletoe with delicate, waxy-white berries was scarce, but it was a best seller. Since mistletoe grew on the highest branches of 100-foot oak trees, it was harvested with a .30-30 rifle. Hiking into the deep woods, finding a large, rare clump, and skillfully shooting the mistletoe stem, made for bragging rights on Main Street.

At the beginning of the season, money was tight, so the biggest limbs of holly were sometimes sold for necessary parking-meter coins. However, just before Christmas, business was so brisk that wreaths were made while customers waited, and trees almost sold out.

Late one Christmas Eve, a well-dressed man hurriedly stopped to look for the "perfect" Christmas tree. He didn't seem to realize that the shapeliest trees had already been sold. It was getting dark, so prices had been reduced—and then slashed—in preparation of closing for the season.

The gentleman became visibly upset and aggravated. He spoke rapidly and loudly with an unfamiliar accent: "Well, I'll just go across the street and buy a Christmas tree bigga, and betta—and cheapa, too!"

The vendor courteously wished the man luck so late on Christmas Eve. But he never forgot about buying something "bigga, and betta—and cheapa, too!" Over the years, it became a favorite saying when someone in the family was looking for a (perhaps non-existent) bargain: "Why don't you just tell them you'll go across the street and buy it bigga, and betta—and cheapa, too!"

During the cold month of December, wind gusts frequently whistled around the corner causing vendors to pull knitted hats lower and collars higher. Snowflakes, promising a white Christmas, settled on the tree display. Still, townsfolk stopped to share a joke, to tell a tall tale, or to wish a Merry Christmas.

Downtown Hendersonville has always been a special place with friendly people.

However, folks were never quite sure if the fellow who boasted of owning "a hammer-handle factory in Missouri" was really a successful entrepreneur. Nevertheless, his stories were entertaining. He was out-going and sociable, like another local man who also frequented Main Street.

He told wonderful tales, too. But he regularly called the White House from the nearest pay phone—loudly demanding to speak directly with President Truman.

When countryfolks sold Christmas greenery on Main Street, they met a lot of other interesting folks. They shared stories, told tall tales, and developed a good number of repeat customers.

Seasonal street businesses supplied the freshest-available decorations for townspeople whose homes were now pleasantly pine-scented for Christmas. The sale of these handcrafts provided money for farm taxes that would be due January 5. And one exceptionally busy December, a vendor paid cash for a New Perfection oil cookstove at Walker's Hardware.

At season's end, country families enjoyed Christmas oranges from the A & P. They always bought "Santa" toys at F.W. Woolworth's 5 and 10 Cent Store, too.

Both were prominent businesses on Main Street back then.

Can you recall Christmas memories of downtown Hendersonville, or of a similar small city? Do you remember some of the old-time stores and the interesting people who made the town so special?

Christmas greenery was sold on Hendersonville's South Main Street for many decades

Decades after countryfolks gathered mountainside greenery to sell from pick-up trucks on Main Street, another thriving seasonal enterprise continued to operate on South Main Street.

At the intersection of the Greenville and Spartanburg Highways, fresh Christmas trees, wreaths, and greenery were sold every December. Admittedly, Fraser Fir trees are thicker, and the wreaths "bigga and betta." Modern families prefer professionally grown greenery—and it is indeed beautiful.

Still, the concept is the same. Seasonal street vendors provide fresh Christmas decorations for townspeople who can't grow their own. Although modern-day artificial trees are designed to appear quite realistic, the market for real trees continues into the 21st century.

During his lifetime, Mr. Cliff Mullinax, Jr., opened the South Main Street business just before Thanksgiving for more than 30 years. Fresh wreaths and decorations were made onsite by employee Raymond Stepp for over 14 years.

These men were quite experienced, and their talent and organizational skills were evident.

Freshly harvested Christmas trees were stunningly displayed on individual stands (instead of leaning on pick-up trucks). Those thick Fraser Firs were grown by a friend, Junior Thomason and his family in Celo, NC, near Burnsville.

Each tree requires at least eight years of professional shaping to grow so tall and beautiful—and this species only thrives in our state's highest elevations. North Carolina agribusiness families, like the Thomasons, have an estimated 50 million Fraser Fir Christmas trees growing on 25,000 acres of steep mountainsides.

With annual arrangements in place for the ideal South Main Street location, Mr. Mullinax didn't need to vie with competitors for the more desirable corners of Hendersonville's Main Street. Modern Christmas lights twinkled over the much-larger parking and display area. This contemporary touch added a cheery glow to the seasonal downtown décor, and loyal customers returned year after year.

Nowadays, any new seasonal street vendors offer better selections of higher-quality trees and decorations than were available in the 1940s. They drive newer and larger transport trucks—and the money they earn isn't as crucial for farm taxes due on January 5.

However, the origins of Christmas trees and handcrafted decorations being sold on Hendersonville's Main Street proudly go back over seven decades.

Townsfolks' homes have continued to be pleasantly pine-scented with natural foliage at Christmas—thanks to modern "countryfolks" who harvest professionally grown greenery from the mountains.

Think about fresh, pine-scented Christmases your family has enjoyed—perhaps from Hendersonville's historic Main Street.

Mr. Ward's Christmas Orange

School principals traditionally have been responsible for shaping lives that eventually shape the community. Especially in the rural South, this local leader often held more than one position at the public school.

As principal at Tuxedo Elementary, Mr. Dean Ward (1904-1991) also taught history, English, geography, and math. Additionally, he played piano and led students in patriotic and folk songs. After making announcements, he seemed to enjoy presenting motivational, assembly speeches to the entire student body.

Our principal tried to instill life lessons in the classroom, as well, and often used examples from his own childhood in Henderson County. During such discourses, he sometimes declared that we "modern, 1950s children" had no idea about hard times.

In his matter-of-fact style, Mr. Ward said even country children were "spoiled and over-privileged" compared to previous generations. Especially at Christmas he wanted students to develop a sense of appreciation for gifts.

*4. Mr. Dean A. Ward (1904-1991) principal
and teacher at Tuxedo Elementary School 1941-1968.*

He knew most kids received toys and new clothes from their parents and that local philanthropists quietly assisted needy families. Green River Mill sponsored an annual party with gift boxes for the children of their 300 - 400 employees, and some employers gave bonuses at Christmas.

Country churches always distributed candy and fruit bags at annual nativity pageants. These bags were commonly called Christmas "pokes" and were generously given to everyone in attendance. This mountain custom, popularized during the Great Depression, was well-known in the early 1950s.

With so many local sources, Mr. Ward knew it was unlikely that a child in his school would be without anything at Christmas. And such knowledge further proved his point.

"Back when I was a little boy," he liked to say, "a big Christmas was when I got an orange." He explained that in the first decades of the 20th century, times had been so hard in the North Carolina mountains, children didn't expect gifts at Christmas.

Yet, holiday traditions of Santa's sleigh, pulled by flying reindeer, had been around almost a century. Known as *The Night before Christmas*, Clement C. Moore's 1823 poem included "eight tiny reindeer" that pranced on the roof when Santa arrived:

...A bundle of toys was flung on his back / And he look'd like a peddler just opening his pack: / His eyes—how they twinkled! His dimples: how merry, / His cheeks were like roses, his nose like a cherry; / He spoke not a word, but went straight to his work, / And fill'd all the stockings then turned with a jerk....

Unfortunately, nearly a hundred years later, story-book fantasies of toys at Christmas were foreign concepts to many mountain children. During Mr. Ward's boyhood in the early 1900s, basics like winter shoes were considered to be luxuries. So, toys from "Santa" certainly weren't anticipated.

In fact, farm families purchased very few items in an era of "Use it up, wear it out, make it do, or do without." Cash money in those days was extremely scarce, so most food was not bought at the country store. Instead, folks ate what was grown on the farm, preserved from the harvest, or hunted in the woods.

In such economic hard times, our school principal had felt very privileged when he received a "store-bought" orange at Christmas. Back then, country grocers in the mountains only ordered oranges in December. So, even families who could afford them rarely enjoyed such treats.

Because such a fine gift wasn't available to Mr. Ward every year, he came to value a Christmas orange even more. "Some Christmases," he recollected, "there just wasn't a present at all."

"The times I received the fresh orange," Mr. Ward explained, "I spent the first few days simply inhaling its rich, citrus fragrance." He described the rusty-yellow-green hue of his childhood orange. (Treatments to produce the bright colors and uniform textures of modern-day fruit hadn't been developed back then.) Slowly and deliberately, he painted word pictures of the thick, nubby hull.

A masterful storyteller and trained teacher, he paused as we visualized scenes of sparse Christmases we had never known. Then, Mr. Ward continued: "By New Year's Day, I'd carefully broken the peel—just enough to remove one juicy segment—while saving the rind."

As a small boy, he relished this delicious slice of Florida sunshine and waited a day or two before eating another wedge. By rationing the Christmas fruit bit by bit, Mr. Ward's treasured gift lasted most of January.

He clarified the reason the orange didn't spoil: He prudently stored it on the windowsill in his cold, unheated bedroom. (Mr. Ward could joke that mountain folks enjoyed mid-winter refrigeration long before electricity became available.)

By carefully preserving the somewhat-bitter peel, he could chew a small, dried piece every day in February. He knew "modern" children wouldn't appreciate such a simple present nor make it last so long—and he told us so.

A full two months past Christmas, the last fragment of his wonderful orange was finally eaten. Mr. Ward finished his story declaring, "I still remember how good that shriveled rind tasted on winter nights in my freezing bedroom."

Coming from such humble beginnings, our principal accomplished a lot in life. His post-graduate English degree made him over-qualified to teach in such a rural area, though his students definitely benefitted.

Mr. Ward, however, was truly glad that times had changed for the better. He enjoyed modern conveniences of a post-war economic boom as much as anyone—but he also recognized the inherent dangers of unchecked prosperity. He wanted us "spoiled, over-privileged" children to realize a basic concept: Even when we have more, appreciation is still a virtue in every generation.

The story of Mr. Ward's Christmas orange has certainly stuck with me for nearly seven decades. I think of him at Christmas and hope each of us who heard his admonitions about gratefulness recalls them, as well.

In memory of those school days, I decorate my Christmas tree with toys I've kept from the generous Green River Mill's gift boxes. The pretty snowman, Santa in his sleigh, a red boot, and stocking continue to be used and celebrated at Christmas.

As one of the "spoiled, over-privileged" country children he exhorted, I looked forward to a Christmas doll. Mama ordered this special gift from the Sears-Roebuck catalog every year. And in the third grade, I lovingly named her Barbara Ann.

When her original, pink-organdy dress faded, Granny sewed a more substantial outfit using recycled, denim fabric from Grandpa's worn-out overalls.

Mr. Ward remembered Christmases much further into the past—hard years like 1910—when an unprocessed orange was special. He wanted students to learn to appreciate gifts, both large and small. Because he foresaw the pitfalls of prosperity, he tried to share his own life lessons and shape our lives for the better.

He believed that gratefulness is a virtue in every generation.

Think about values, in addition to reading, writing, and arithmetic, that were imparted by your early teachers.

Can you recall family stories about sparse Christmases during your grandparents' childhoods?

Were there times when you delighted in simple Christmas presents—even though they may have been less expensive (and fewer) than would be customary today?

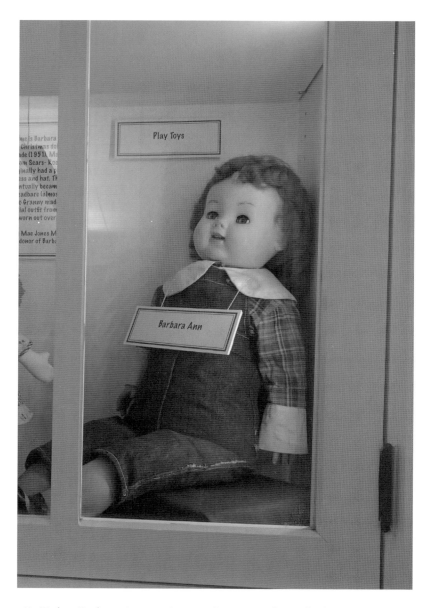

5. *Today, Barbara Ann continues to be treasured in a display in Mountain Heritage Center Museum at Western Carolina University. With my metal tea set, and the rag and corncob dolls Granny designed, the Christmas doll represents that long-ago era just after World War II.*

Christmas plays and Christmas "pokes" at country churches

Southern churches were initially slow to incorporate Christmas into their order of worship. Secular celebrations on December 25th were typically rowdy and were to be avoided. Besides, folks still favored Old Christmas on January 6th and thought of December 25th as the "new" Christmas. By the 1830s, however, churches gradually began using nativity scenes in conjunction with the "new" Christmas. Particularly after the Civil War, reenactments of Mary, Joseph, and the Christ child began to be accepted as a way to promote Christianity.

In the early years of the 20th century, the tradition became more established in the South. Typically scheduled the Sunday night before Christmas or oftentimes Christmas Eve night, the annual pageant became a standing-room-only event. Other than Homecoming, it was the biggest gathering of the year.

Sunday School teachers, musicians, and the pastor's wife worked together to plan the annual Christmas play. Without budgeted funds, they had to use imagination and creativity. Volunteers would hammer together a wooden stable and bring an actual manger with hay from someone's barn. Families tended to be large back then, so there usually wasn't a problem finding a newborn and his parents for the manger scene. Sunday School children could play the parts of shepherds and wise men. Pastors knew that kinfolk who didn't usually attend church would come to see little Billy in his costume.

6. Zion Hill Baptist Church in Zirconia, continued the Southern tradition of annual Christmas plays followed by the distribution of Christmas "pokes." This manger scene from previous years shows their dedication to sharing the Good News of the birth of the Christ child.

Country churches, particularly in Appalachia, used what they had to create those costumes and backdrops. Even in my childhood, I recall sheets pinned to clotheslines and stretched across the platform for stage curtains. Children looked quite properly attired in costumes of wool scarves, towels, and blankets tied with ropes, and they sometimes carried shepherds' staffs whittled from tree limbs. If nothing else was available, crowns could be cut from "pasteboard" boxes and trimmed with buttons. Mountain ladies have a long history of creatively "making do."

7. Costumes for Christmas pageants have evolved since the Great Depression. Worn by Larry McKinley, this kingly robe was created by Mrs. Pat Sanders.

In practice sessions, Sunday School teachers patiently demonstrated when to walk down the aisle and where to stand. Pint-sized wise men learned to kneel as they offered gifts of older sisters' gilded jewelry boxes to the Christ child. Then, at the actual pageant, proud grandparents nodded and smiled at little Johnny's almost-flawless performance.

The Pastor read appropriate scriptures from St. Matthew and St. Luke, and the congregation joined in the carol-singing. *O, come all ye faith-ful, joy-ful and tri-um-phant....*

was an anthem to the crowds who had walked from miles around, oftentimes in snow. During the 1930s, few folks could afford to drive even if they'd bought a car before the Great Depression. But everybody wanted to come, even if they couldn't sing very well and weren't participating in the play.

Aside from the intended spiritual benefits, nativity pageants in these isolated mountains were the most popular social gatherings to wish friends a Merry Christmas. It was a time to greet cousins from Bob's Creek, Cedar Springs, and Mt. Olivet—and many a romance sparked as visiting young folks found the Love of their Life in a crowded church aisle on Christmas Eve.

During the hard years of the Great Depression, country churches introduced a new tradition. Using what money they scraped together from the treasury, they managed to order boxes of penny candy, mixed nuts, apples, and oranges. Usually one of the deacons owned the local country store and could offer wholesale prices.

During my childhood, Mr. Than Maybin served his church, Crossroads Baptist, from Maybin's Grocery in Zirconia. *(See the photo in the story about shopping in a country store.)* Mr. U.S. Staton of Staton's Grocery and Mr. Lum Pace of M.C. Pace's Grocery did the same for churches in the Green River community. Country stores were common back then, so most area congregations had access to generous wholesale pricing. In Saluda, another Mr. Pace served churches through his already-historic M.A. Pace General Store.

Before the pageant, deacons would meet with the Pastor to pack maybe two or three hundred lunch-size paper "pokes" with fruit, nuts, and candy. These treat-filled bags would be piled high on the back pews ready to be distributed as folks left the Christmas play.

8. Members of Scenic Hills Baptist Church pack fruit, nuts, and candy "pokes" to be distributed at the Christmas play.

Like other mountain expressions, the word "poke" came from the old countries. France, Germany, England and Scotland have versions of the term dating back to the 1200s and earlier. *Poki, poket, poque, pokete* and *pouche* were gradually assimilated into the more common English words like pocket, poke, and pouch. Rather than being "incorrect," the mountain expression, "poke" was really an Old English word.

It is thought-provoking to recall that during the 1930s, the U.S. unemployment rate averaged 25 percent, and in Appalachia it was even higher. Mountain folks were considered to be poor before the Great Depression, so a running joke was, "What depression?"

At Christmas no one expected much, so receiving a treat-filled bag by going to a play they probably already planned to attend seemed almost magical. Apples were grown on the farm, but oranges were so special that mountain grocers only ordered them in December. Even the few families who could afford high-priced citrus fruit could only buy it at Christmas when it became available at country stores.

For most mountain children, an orange, a store-bought apple, and a whole handful of nuts and penny candy was a fabulous Christmas. These generous church gifts were often-times all they and their entire families received. Children were familiar with mountain walnuts, but the mixed nuts in a Christmas "poke" were quite exotic. Pecans, Hazelnuts, and Brazil nuts tasted different and special.

Then, they dug down to the candy pieces sprinkled in the bottom. In my childhood, Christmas "pokes" included candy-orange slices, peppermint sticks with red stripes, multi-colored hard candies, and my favorite chocolate drops bursting with vanilla-crème. To me it was all delicious, but for a child of the Great Depression who had literally not tasted candy nor citrus since last Christmas, the gift of a "poke" was breathtaking.

Hard-working farmers who could not provide gifts for their children must have been relieved and grateful for the benevolence of the local church. Now, their families had a good Christmas during a world-wide financial depression. In my childhood, I recall deacons following folks down the church steps asking, "Did you get a "poke?" Those good men didn't want visitors or homefolks to be left out of the church's generosity.

None of the "pokes" went to waste, either. The Pastor had a list of elderly and "shut-in" folks that he and the dea-cons delivered to before Christmas. They made frequent announcements for church members to take extra bags to sick neighbors and kinfolks.

And a few country churches still carry on this tradition in the 21st century. Nowadays, most recipients don't need fruit and candy bags quite as desperately as the mountain people of the 1930s. Still, elderly homebound folks are thrilled to be remembered by their local church. A "poke" brings back warm Christmas memories to many older people. They recall such generous gifts in the hard years of the Great Depression.

During the 2020 Coronavirus pandemic, it is less likely that churches will continue their once-packed-out Christmas pageants. Standing-room-only gatherings could become "super-spreader" events these days. However, with modern communications, churches can plan online programs and amplified drive-in services that retell the story of the Christ child's birth. Deacons and Pastors can still deliver fruit and candy to the elderly—and the Christmas season can continue to be celebrated.

Think about Christmas pageants you attended or participated in as a child. Recall your costume, especially if it was homemade. Were you familiar with country churches that provided "pokes" at the Christmas play?

9. The M.A. Pace General Store opened in 1899 on Saluda's Main Street. Under the new ownership of Mr. Leon Morgan, a relative of the Pace family, it continues to operate in the 21ˢᵗ century.

Granny ate black-eyed peas on New Year's and observed Old Christmas on January 6

10. On New Year's Day, many people in the South ate this traditional dinner for success in the coming year.

On Bear Mountain, January was a special month with two important dates to be honored in the traditions of the South. On New Year's Day, Granny always cooked black-eyed peas, turnip greens, and cornbread. According to folklore, eating that meal on New Year's would bring good luck throughout the entire year. Old folks said the peas represented copper coins, and turnip greens foretold green, folding money. Even their favorite golden-brown cornbread meant lots of gold in the coming year.

Of course, no one really believed in the actual monetary effect, but the meal was "a mighty tasty way to start off a new year," according to Grandpa.

And Granny always cooked what Grandpa liked.

Flavored with fatback meat, the peas simmered on the back of the woodstove all morning. They were easily ready in time for the midday meal because they'd been soaked overnight (actually since last year).

In another large iron pot, a "mess" of turnip greens steamed in their own fatback-laden "potlicker." Other Southern ladies used mustard greens or collards since the custom seemed to center around availability rather than a special kind of greens.

Closer to mealtime, Granny heated more fatback grease in an iron skillet in the woodstove oven to bake a thick "pone" of crusty cornbread. Just as Grandpa was seated, she ceremoniously flipped the bread—still steaming—onto a platter in the middle of the table.

Country people didn't just politely nibble little corn sticks like modern folks. They broke off hunks of hot cornbread and crumbled it in the juicy "potlicker" of both the greens and black-eyed peas. Like Grandpa said, the meal was "a mighty tasty way to start off a new year."

Granny and Grandpa observed the Southern tradition with good humor, and I remember countryfolks' lighthearted greetings well into the month of January: "Well, did you eat your turnip greens and black-eyed peas on New Year's Day?"

Very few would admit to not following the legendary custom. So, the answer was laughingly given in the affirmative: "You know we wouldn't miss having our turnip greens and black-eyed peas. We're looking forward to making lots of money all year."

My grandparents wouldn't have known the actual history of the tradition. But they would have appreciated the celebratory tribute and the story of endurance.

Black-eyed peas really did bring good fortune to former slaves and survivors of the Civil War. When General Sherman marched across Georgia to the sea, his army consumed or destroyed crops, livestock, and stored resources.

However, the black-eyed peas were left because they were food for livestock—and the soldiers had already captured or eaten the animals. Thinking the peas were worthless, the army ignored them and completed their rampage to the coast by the end of December 1864. As the people came out of hiding and looked toward the new year of 1865, they cooked the tasty, nutritious black-eyed peas.

The "worthless" peas were indeed healthful: A one-cup serving is low in calories and carbohydrates, but high in fiber and protein. Black-eyed peas are also rich in vitamins A, C, E, K, B_6, Thiamin, Riboflavin, Niacin, Folate, Calcium, Iron, and Magnesium.

If the General had only known....

The people felt so blessed that beginning on New Year's Day in 1866, the custom of eating black-eyed peas was celebrated in honor of survival, for the end of the war—and in hope for a brighter new year.

That joyful commemoration continues today throughout the South.

Around Christmastime, local grocery stores begin featuring up-front displays of various kinds of fresh greens, along with fatback, and black-eyed peas. They know customers want to shop in time to prepare the traditional New Year's Day meal.

Southern folks still celebrate the old ways—and we still look forward to a good year ahead.

Can you recall good-humored New Year's greetings, or perhaps eating the customary meal at an older relative's home?

Granny always said January 6 was the real Christmas

She talked a lot about the days when "Old Christmas" was quietly and reverently observed on January 6. She considered December 25, along with Santa and his reindeer, to be the "modern" Christmas. For the grandchildren's sake, though, she did go along with some of the popular festivities.

Still, Granny held to her lifelong belief in the "real" Christmas on January 6.

She would not have known that the idea went back to at least 534 A. D.

At that time January 6, the Day of Epiphany, began to be celebrated as the date of the coming of the Magi to worship the Christ child. December 25 was celebrated as the feast of Christmas, and the days between those dates became known as the Twelve Days of Christmas.

If Granny was familiar with the children's song, *The Twelve Days of Christmas*, she would not have connected it to the two Christmas dates.

The Old-World tradition of Christmas on January 6 had indeed crossed the ocean with the first settlers. Granny's ancestors came from Great Britain—where the people had loudly protested the Calendar Act of 1751. British citizens of that era resisted the change to the Gregorian calendar that removed eleven days from the reckoning of a year.

Traditionally, they had celebrated Christmas on January 6—and they continued to do so even after the Gregorian calendar became the standard by which dates were determined.

By the new calendar Christmas Day was celebrated on December 25, and the British people of the 1700s stubbornly defied the change.

Some of their descendants in the North Carolina mountains, like my Granny, still didn't like it two hundred years later.

She said she'd always heard that barn animals knelt at midnight on January 5, in honor of the Christ child being born in their stable. Another mountain legend declares that sheep, cows, and donkeys remember the Baby Jesus. So, they pray at midnight, using their own voices, to honor His birth on January 6.

On Bear Mountain, Granny kept the old ways alive, and she made sure I knew about the tradition.

She always said young people ought to appreciate the customs of the old days—and I think it is important and thought-provoking to listen to older people. Their rich heritage encompasses eras that are history-book material now.

Old Christmas on January 6 was a tradition that went back in time—all the way to the Old Country.

Few in our modern world would have ever heard of it.

It might be interesting to talk with the oldest person you know and ask if their parents or grandparents observed Old Christmas.

Paper dolls nurture imagination during snowy winters

11. In the late 1940s and early 1950s, Janie Mae recalls playing with paper dolls on the rosy living-room floor in her grandmother's home. A popular linoleum design of the era featured ever-blooming roses on a burgundy background. A recreated fireside scene shows vintage paper dolls, including a pink-gowned bridal party, displayed on a similar rose-patterned floor.

Little girls in the mountains enjoyed playing with paper dolls during long, winter afternoons, especially before the advent of television. As light snow settled on hilltop trees, I remember sitting on the flowery linoleum floor beside the wood heater. The cheery, ever-blooming-rose pattern on the flooring spread across the entire living room. Those summer roses and glowing-hot fires in Granny's 1895 farmhouse contradicted the cold, outside temperatures and the coming snow.

Being warm and quite content, I focused attention on the intricate art of using scissors to neatly trim the paper costumes. Such careful effort was essential, so the elaborate gowns would look good on the cardboard dolls. Unlike real girls and ladies that I knew, the glamorous people featured in cut-out books wore high-fashion clothes every day—and every evening. The era of the late 1940s and early 1950s is included in "The Golden Age of Paper Dolls," so I had many delightful choices.

Their enduring popularity was partly a result of advancing print technology in the late 19th and early 20th centuries. Manufacturing costs decreased at approximately the same time brighter, color-copy techniques increased. Thus, beautifully colored (but inexpensive) paper dolls became available.

The booklets featured movie stars, models, and beautiful brides with dozens of interchangeable paper gowns and dresses in every color of the rainbow. Their painted-on hair was luxuriantly black or golden blonde with lipstick-red lips, bright eyes, and artistically long eyelashes. Admittedly, they were two-dimensional cardboard. But with a little imagination, the dolls enjoyed changing into colorful play outfits after attending make-believe dances and parties. Their stylish winter coats—with matching red hats and muffs—were still waiting to be cut from the latest paper-doll book.

A particular favorite was the cardboard bride who wore a lavish pink gown. Her matron of honor, bridesmaid, and flower girl were also dressed in flowing pink costumes. Of course, I had never seen a pink wedding gown, but no one else had, either. (It was likely shown in pastels to make the booklet more attractive.) Pink was my favorite color, so I spent many happy hours clipping paper gowns and pretend pink bouquets.

Known as "America's Sweetheart," the child star Shirley Temple began her acting career at age three. She sang and danced through dozens of movies while girls her age were still in elementary school. Because of continued popularity, her paper dolls were treasured and reprinted after the real, curly-haired girl had grown up. My cardboard Shirley never outgrew fancy dresses or sailor suits—and she certainly never wore hand-me-downs like children I knew. Pages of elaborate movie costumes could be cut and folded around her adorable likeness. Posing on the rosy floor, even after multiple outfit changes, Shirley was always smiling and happy. And she certainly brought joy and happiness to me on long winter afternoons.

Even in those days, paper dolls were considered old-fashioned, having been manufactured since the early 1800s. However, along with Shirley Temple, they had come into their own during the Great Depression. Because paper dolls were cheaper than real dolls, mothers could stretch limited resources further. Since the only other requirement was an old pair of dull scissors, paper fashions offered fun and imaginative flights-of-fancy during hard times.

Through the 1950s, the colorful booklets continued to be a popular staple at F.W. Woolworth's 5 & 10 Cent Store on Hendersonville's Main Street. Several generations of young girls anticipated the latest high-fashion issues.

It is thought that cardboard dolls were intentionally designed to reflect the expectations and aspirations of girls and women in a particular era. Like most toys, they encouraged girls in the fantasies of role playing, though those roles were defined by the wardrobe choices. Over time, the costumes began to depict career women as well as "ladies of leisure" who spent their days and evenings at social events.

For younger girls, the appeal was the extensive wardrobes and possibilities of life choices that may not have been available to women in previous generations. Knowingly or unknowingly, a lady made statements about herself and her sense of identity through the clothing styles she chose. Ordinary people wore clothes, but not everybody wore fashion, so playing with paper dolls gave girls a safe view into other women's lives.

Brides with numerous bridesmaids (like the pink-gowned wedding party) remained popular since the concept of a dream wedding was consistent over time. Some wedding cut-out books, however, neglected to include the groom and his attendants. Rather than an oversight, companies may have thought dark suits and tuxedos just weren't colorful enough to take up so many pages. After all, each beautifully gowned bridesmaid required an extra groomsman in the make-believe, paper-doll wedding. Sitting beside the glowing wood heater on winter afternoons, my cardboard dolls and I arranged those large, elaborate weddings.

And we enjoyed trips to the beach in stylish bathing costumes. To prevent imaginary sunburn, the dolls donned matching terrycloth coverups and wide, floppy hats. Quite conveniently, we'd brought them along in coordinating beach bags.

Tiring of sand and surf, we attended lavish balls while wearing evening gowns that glittered in the starlight. The enchanting paper dolls whirled and waltzed across the rose-patterned floor; their dance steps seemed to follow strains of orchestra music I'd heard on the battery radio. While I played so happily, child star Shirley Temple never grew up. Her curly hair stayed in curls, and her ruffled dresses fit perfectly. And pages of gowns waited to be cut, with more adventure stories to be imagined.

Meanwhile, on my grandparents' secluded mountain, the afternoon snow continued to fall, softly, steadily and silently. Back from the dolls' pretend day at the beach, I watched from the window as snow mounded over the box-woods. They looked like huge coconut cakes covered with Granny's tasty 7-Minute Icing, but I was glad to be inside by the warm fire.

The concept of imagination in child development remains as important today as it was decades ago. Actually, some modern amusements are thought to hinder children from using natural creative skills. It is interesting to real-ize that old-fashioned playthings, favored during the Great Depression were so beneficial.

Many of my treasured childhood paper dolls are displayed at Mountain Heritage Center Museum on the campus of Western Carolina University. Along with other donated antiques, they are used in education programs to familiarize modern children with the past.

Today, I live on Bear Mountain, still enjoy wood fires on snowy afternoons—and collect sets of vintage paper dolls. Decades later, cardboard dolls with glamorous paper ward-robes have not lost their fascinating appeal. And I find that other older ladies remember and enjoy the challenging fun activity, as well. Carefully trimming the dolls and dressing them in colorful gowns is still entertaining.

Ask an older lady friend or relative if she recalls playing with paper dolls as a young girl. She may remember their fashionable clothing styles—as well as imaginative stories she made up about their adventures.

Think about other toys you especially enjoyed that would be considered outdated today. Looking back to snowy winter afternoons in your childhood, envision the solitude, the tranquility, and the pleasures of simple amusements and imagination.

Shopping in a country store was a social event

U nlike today when we dash into a supermarket to pick up a few things for dinner, shopping in a country store was a social event. On Saturday mornings in the late 1940s and early 1950s, Grandpa walked two miles down the mountain to Maybin's Grocery in Zirconia.

Going to the store was the way he kept up with the local news. Without telephones or close neighbors, mountain folks routinely gathered at country stores for news and socialization.

Mr. Than Maybin's store seemed to be especially suited for visiting as well as shopping. Conveniently located on U.S. Hwy. 25, next to the train station, and across the tracks from the Post Office, it had a steady stream of customers.

Built to hang out over a deep gully, the spacious store and live-in apartment was constructed of neatly painted white boards. Next to the parking lot, a wide, covered veranda sheltered the gas pumps.

Not that it mattered much to Grandpa, but the price of gasoline was 26.9¢ a gallon. Since there were no roads to Bear Mountain, he'd never considered the possibility of learning to drive.

12. This photograph is of Mr. Than Maybin's Grocery in Zirconia, NC decades before he owned it. It is likely that the couple posing in front of the store were the proprietors in the 1920s - 1930s. Notice the gasoline pumps underneath the porch, the antique cars, and the Tuxedo train station in the background beside the railroad tracks. (Neither of these historical buildings continue to exist in the 21st century.)

Inside the well-kept store, locals played checkers, swapped knives, and told tales as they warmed around the pot-bellied stove in colder weather. Strong fumes from Hav-A-Tampa cigars threatened to fill the room. The men puffed and then used their lit cigars to gesture as they recounted hunting and trapping exploits: "That mink was so big…."

Grandpa politely greeted the fellows who were sitting around the stove, and they chorused, "Howdy, Mr. Russell," "Mornin' Uncle Will." Though it was unlikely they were related, the respectful use of Uncle to address an elderly man was an old-fashioned Southern custom.

Grandpa chatted with them and with Mr. Maybin as he caught up on the news and drank a Coke. In the words of a vintage Coca-Cola advertisement, they became a part of "America's Friendliest Neighborhood Club...Admission 5¢."

In fact, gathering at country stores to socialize with a 5¢ glass-bottled, soft drink was so customary that parking lots were often "paved" with the discarded tops. On the front of the drink cooler, a pop-off opener held maybe a day's worth of bottle caps. Then, country store owners like Mr. Maybin dumped them outside to serve as quite-substantial, free gravel.

Before the era of self-serve stores with wide aisles, shopping carts, and eye-level shelves, customers asked for each item they bought. The system worked quite well, since the proprietor was often the only one who knew where to find groceries stacked on high, wall shelves. In the process, shoppers gathered information because the store owner took time to discuss the advantages of one brand over another.

In a small community, he also knew the customers well enough to help them choose items they could use. Over the years a successful store owner learned to listen and remember information without being obvious. For example, Mr. Maybin would have known if a family didn't have a refrigerator at home and discreetly not have suggested foods that would spoil before they could be used.

At Grandpa's direction, Mr. Maybin began piling groceries on the counter. He included brands he recommended as well as those Grandpa especially wanted because they were advertised on *Art Linkletter's House Party* or the *Grand Ole Opry*: Maxwell House coffee, Carnation canned milk, 99 $^{44}/_{100}$% pure Ivory soap, Nabisco saltine crackers, Campbell's soup, and Martha White Self-Rising Flour (with the highly advertised ingredient, Hotrize).

This personal interaction between the customer and the owner of the store created bonds of lifelong friendship in small mountain communities. Grandpa considered Mr.

Maybin as a friend as well as a local businessman, and their respect and appreciation was mutual.

Shopping wasn't simply purchasing food and necessities; it was a social event, a morning away from farm chores, a time to catch up with the news—and a chance to visit with friends over a 5¢ Coke.

Remember an old-fashioned store where your grandparents shopped and how much a soft drink cost in those days. It might be interesting to compare that level of social interaction with our hurried lifestyle and our impatience when we wait in long checkout lines.

13. Wall mural by Bruce Zior in the Red Hill community near Loafers Glory, North Carolina. The painting covers the outside wall of Red Hill Convenience Store and recalls the original grocery that opened at that location in 1915. Businesses like Red Hill Store were typical in North Carolina's mountains during the early to mid-1900s. Local men regularly gathered to play checkers, tell tall tales, and swap knives.

Tall tales, checkers, and knife swapping at the country store

Particularly during cold, winter months, farmers and other local men enjoyed walking to the country store. Most people didn't have telephones or radios, and there was no television back then, so the store became a community center. In addition to visiting, the fellows could catch up on news, bemoan bad weather, tell tall tales, play checkers, and swap knives.

The more fortunate, who had new-fangled, battery radios at home, could share the national news with the group. Folks were interested in what President Franklin Roosevelt said, even though Washington seemed to be a world away from the mountains of North Carolina.

However, almanac weather predictions were relied on more than radio weather reports, since farmers planted crops by the signs of the moon. Exactly when to begin plowing made for lively discussions when men were already getting cabin fever.

In January, the once-brown fields were white, laurel leaves curled against the cold, and icicles dangled from eves. The snow had come often and uninvited, and it didn't want to leave.

Even in modern times, older folks declare that winters were colder in those days. For farmers looking forward to turning furrows in the garden, it seemed that spring would never come.

But it was pleasant to pass midwinter afternoons around the potbellied stove with neighbors and kinfolks. Everybody knew everybody else, and most were distantly related. On such cold days, genealogy was always an interesting topic. Figuring out whose grandma's sister had been married to Great-Uncle Josh's cousin could fill hours of "loafing" time.

In fact, Loafers Glory, North Carolina, is a real community in Mitchell County near the Tennessee state line. It was supposedly named by neighborhood ladies who thought their husbands were spending too much time at the country store.

The Red Hill Store, not far from Loafers Glory, was also a well-known gathering place years ago. Merchants like U.S. Staton, Than Maybin, and Lum Pace in Henderson County, along with M.C. Pace in Saluda, operated businesses much like the original Loafers Glory Grocery. Such stores regularly attracted loafers who told tales, played checkers, and swapped knives. And these activities were usually accompanied by hefty "chaws" from twists of home-grown chewing tobacco.

Fumes from popular Hav-A-Tampa cigars sometimes threatened to fill the room. Men puffed and used their lit cigars to gesture as they recounted hunting and trapping exploits: "That mink was s-o-o-o big...." More smoke billowed toward the ceiling as the stove door was occasionally opened to pitch in more coal or wood.

Some fellows could be described as "professional loafers" since they were consistently unemployed. But times had been hard, so they were accepted into the group of local farmers who were simply waiting for spring.

The store proprietor didn't expect to sell much to these all-day loafers, but they kept him company. Very few paying customers came to the store on cold, mid-week afternoons, so he often joined the checker playing around the stove.

In such a public place, the red and black wooden checkers eventually became lost. Fortunately, popular glass-bottled, soft drinks featured red or black metal caps. These were saved and used for checkerboard pieces, and they worked as well as the originals.

14. *Leon Morgan (pictured on left) owner of M. A. Pace General Store in Saluda, plays checkers with Janie Mae's brother, James Evance Jones. Reminiscent of fellows in years past, they are "loafing" around a potbellied stove display at the old-time store. Notice that the checker pieces are bottle caps from soft drinks (a common innovation when checkers were lost at a country store).*

Actually, champion players developed in these community gathering spots. There were stories of fellows who learned to anticipate three or four moves across the checkerboard. As local experts, they eventually qualified for area competitions.

Others just excelled in telling tall tales. When one of my Jones ancestors told a "whopper" folks declared, "Now, Uncle Trammel, you know that wasn't the way it really happened." His Appalachian-English response to their teasing was, "Of course not, but it shore makes a good story, don't it?"

Everybody enjoyed the tale about a "local" farmer who was hoeing the garden when a rattlesnake bit the hoe handle. The wooden handle swelled so much that he sawed enough lumber from it to build a pigpen.

Unfortunately, when the swelling went down, the pigpen shrank—and strangled all his pigs.

In such tall tales, mountain mosquitos were "real big." One farmer tied his plow horses in the shade while he walked home for dinner. By the time he got back, the mosquitos had eaten both horses—and were tossing the horseshoes to see who would eat him.

In those early decades of the 1900s, folks still recalled stories of wild panthers roaming the mountains. Harrowing experiences of being stalked and chased hadn't passed from living memory (though a few details may have been embellished over the years).

An almost-believable version was somebody's grandma who lived alone in the woods. While bringing in night wood, she heard the scream of a panther. Running, slamming and bolting the door, she felt secure until the growling "painter" snarled through cracks in the cabin floor.

Instead of panicking, she calmly added the wood to the fireplace flames and heated a kettle of water. Just as sharp claws began ripping floorboards—with eyes glowing in the firelight—she doused him with scalding water.

Panthers "screamed like a woman" anyway. In this story, the wounded panther fled through the forest with ear-splitting shrieks that could be heard for miles. The elderly lady had been shaken, but safe, because of quick thinking and mountain resourcefulness.

Such terrifying encounters could have happened when settlers first came to Henderson County. So, afternoon patrons around the stove nodded with approval at her bravery and ingenuity.

Knife swapping also provided entertainment for everyone in the room, even if they weren't trading knives that day. Men always carried a good pocketknife, along with an extra to swap for perhaps a better knife. From force of habit, and to demonstrate its trade-worthiness, they often whittled as they sat around the stove.

So many swaps were made, it was possible to end up with the knife they brought. Such a probability created a round of guffawing, along with good-natured teasing.

Time passed quite agreeably in their community of longtime friendships and camaraderie. But midwinter days were short. The sun was setting, and it didn't look like there'd been any snowmelt all day.

Old-timers joked that January's temperature had to climb to single digits—and the store's Coca-Cola advertising thermometer showed it was already dropping. Farm chores were waiting, with wood and water to be carried before dark.

The fellows who had walked the farthest needed to start toward home. They might get a ride with one of the locals, though evening rush-hour traffic didn't exist back then.

In fact, the concept of rushing to any place was unknown. Very few vehicles traveled the recently paved U.S. Highway 25, and even fewer on gravel roads.

In an era before television, when telephones and electricity weren't generally available, country stores provided a sense of connection. Mountain ladies may have considered the whole lot of them to be in "loafers' glory," but such community gathering places remained popular.

You may have heard some tall tales and legendary stories that were once told at country stores.

When visiting older friends or kinfolks, ask about their memories of long, winter afternoons before television. They may be familiar with knife swapping, and checkers could have been a game they enjoyed, as well.

Think about small grocery stores you remember—and the interesting people who frequented them.

Poke the groceries in a bag or bag them in a poke?

15. *Mr. Leon Morgan, present-day owner of M. A. Pace General Store in Saluda, poses with "a poke of penny candy." He maintains the 1899 heritage of the store and continues to provide brown paper "pokes" for customers, along with displays of individual candy pieces.*

When Grandpa walked two miles to Maybin's Grocery, he didn't always need the paper bags supplied by country grocers. Instead of using paper "pokes" (as he called them), he brought a neatly folded, cotton feed sack in his overalls pocket.

A hundred pounds of cow feed was, by necessity, packaged in heavy-duty cotton sacks. Thrifty mountain folks repurposed them as large, tough, grocery bags.

Grandpa was ahead of his time.

Green living, recycling, and reusable, fabric shopping bags aren't just modern concepts. Country people like Grandpa reused almost everything, and he certainly preferred carrying heavy groceries in a sturdy bag.

Hiking home from the store (uphill in all kinds of weather) was hard enough without worrying about the bottoms falling out of multiple paper bags. Groceries would have spilled beside the railroad tracks, in the creek, and all along the trail on his way back to Bear Mountain.

Between regular shopping trips, Grandpa would tolerate paper bags for just a few items. The mountain name "poke" was so familiar, store owners sometimes joked, "Should I poke these groceries in a bag, or bag them in a poke?"

The end result was the same because plastic grocery bags hadn't been invented back then. Nobody had ever heard the modern question, "Would you like paper or plastic?"

Glass bottles were appropriately packaged in durable paper bags at liquor stores, so creative Southerners named them "poke stores." Such purchases were sometimes "disguised" in those same bags while the alcohol was being consumed. This practice provoked many a country woman to snipe, "Well, I see that you stopped at that ole poke store on the way home!"

Appalachian children considered "a nickel poke of penny candy" to be a special treat. On those exciting occasions,

I remember gazing through the thick glass at the candy counter. From the colorful—and almost overwhelming—display, I carefully chose exactly five pieces:

A candy orange slice, one peppermint stick, two chocolate drops, and a Tootsie roll. Mr. Maybin, the busy grocer, dutifully filled the five-cent order and graciously handed me the little "poke."

Country folks typically lived several miles from the nearest town. So, any visitor from afar who remembered to bring "a poke of penny candy for the young'uns" was welcome indeed.

In fact, the only gifts some mountain families received were Christmas "pokes" distributed at nativity pageants. Those fruit and candy bags guaranteed that the church would be filled the night of the annual play. Men, women, and children were generously included in the distribution. As folks were leaving, the deacons always asked, "Did you get a poke?"

Like Grandpa's cloth feed sacks, paper "pokes" were recycled as well. Granny found multiple uses for them around the house. They were handy for fire starters, though book covers were once very popular.

During the Great Depression, schools couldn't afford supplies, so textbooks had to be purchased by parents. Brown-paper jackets helped keep expensive books nice enough to be resold the following year to younger students.

Paper bags could also be used to carry mail, store jar lids, garden seeds, or dried walnuts. As temporary hothouses, they protected tender garden plants and flowers during late-spring frosts.

Mountain girls learned to cut paper "pokes" into strips to curl their hair for special occasions.

These free grocery sacks made good writing paper for lists, letters, or homework. Rainy-day art activities included drawing, coloring, or designing paper dolls. Before movie-themed Halloween costumes, a decorated paper bag with eyes, nose, and mouth cut-outs was quite scary.

Brown "poke" paper was commonly used for giftwrapping, making homemade Christmas-tree decorations, and as package filling (before Styrofoam peanuts). It was not unusual to see brown-bag wallpaper in mountain homes or wadded-paper insulation around door or window frames to protect against winter drafts.

Bureau drawers and kitchen shelves could be lined for free, and instead of modern paper towels, handy "pokes" absorbed extra grease from country-fried chicken. (After that use, they made excellent fire starters.)

Before school cafeterias or insulated lunch containers, mountain children carried leftover biscuits and fatback to school in "pokes" or paper sugar bags.

Brown paper was useful to cut a watermelon on, or to set underneath a dripping paint can. Gathering a mess of snap beans from the garden was a snap with a couple of paper "pokes."

When hot food needed to be delivered to a neighbor, a few layers of grocery-bag paper assured that it would arrive at the desired temperature. After electricity became available, ice was regularly wrapped in multiple brown bags to share with neighbors.

It has been said that "Necessity is the mother of invention," and folks were quite imaginative in finding uses for thick, free, "poke" paper.

In the 1940s and early 1950s, country people still described almost any paper bag as a "poke." On those long-ago Saturdays, I remember Grandpa asking Granny what she needed from the store. In addition to other groceries, she'd often include, "a poke of sugar, and a poke of cornmeal."

Times were changing, though, and the name was becoming outdated.

However, as with many other mountain expressions, the word "poke" came from the old countries. France, Germany, England, and Scotland have versions of the term dating back to the 1200s and earlier. *Poki, poket, poque, pokete,* and *pouche* were gradually assimilated into more-common English words like pocket, "poke," and pouch.

Larger "pokes," once made of leather (but more often of heavy fabric) were traditionally used for a variety of purposes. They were convenient for transporting pigs to the market, hence the adage, "Don't buy a pig in a poke."

Deceitful farmers sometimes substituted cats or puppies for edible rabbits or piglets. So, as early as 1530, honest traders in London were advised, "When ye proffer the pigge, open the poke."

The first paper-bag machine was eventually patented in 1852. Then, the centuries-old word "poke" came to describe disposable bags, as well. Even today, candy purchased in Scotland is often carried home in a small paper sack they call a "poke bag." The bonny Scots also describe a container of French fries as a "poke o' chips," or a "poke" of chips.

It is interesting that this colorful, old-world term is still used. During my Southern grandparents' lifetimes, it was becoming archaic, oddly Appalachian, and maybe a little peculiar.

But words brought directly from the old countries would sound different, and expressions sometimes remained unchanged for generations. Now, they can provide insight into our ancestors' diverse and fascinating cultural backgrounds.

Had you ever heard the old-fashioned saying, "Don't buy a pig in a poke?" Think about other idioms or unique words that may have come from ancestral homelands.

Even though you may have known it by a different name, can you remember when "a poke of penny candy" was a special treat?

Recall some of the ingenious ways your older relatives reused paper bags or feed sacks—years before recycling became widely accepted.

Before electricity, "coal-oil" lamps glimmered in mountain farmhouses

At the turn of the 20th century, electricity was a new phenomenon, and electric lights were a marvel in the mountains of Western North Carolina. Electricity first came to Hendersonville in 1903, and prospective manufacturers also needed electrical service. By 1907, new textile mills in East Flat Rock and Tuxedo had means of generating electricity. The companies brought jobs and electric lighting to those fortunate communities.

Other rural neighborhoods in Henderson County gradually received access to electricity, some sooner, and others much later. Mountain people have always been resourceful, so a few talented families produced electricity from nearby creeks before it became commercially available. Others purchased propane refrigerators, cookstoves, and lights, and I remember attending a country church that used gas camping lanterns to illuminate the sanctuary.

When I was a child in the late 1940s and early 1950s, remote areas of Henderson County hadn't been included in the general network of power poles and electric lines. Sparsely populated communities needed a reasonable number of households to qualify, so the electrical requirements of summer camps and vacation homes helped fund new lines across the mountains.

Still, electricity was not available on Bear Mountain during Grandpa's lifetime. That area was so remote it lacked even a road until 1975. Electrical service quickly followed once the vicinity became accessible and more populated with contemporary housing developments.

So, Granny and Grandpa used "coal-oil" lamps decades after communities just across their mountain had been connected to electricity. The first thing most Appalachian families got rid of was their oil lamps when electricity became available. In the mid-1950s, such lamps seemed old-fashioned and out of date, though my grandparents considered them adequate for their needs.

16. Country Hawkins lights a hanging, oil lamp in his kitchen. He is well prepared for ice storms and power outages. His family lived so far from town, electricity only became available in 1949, and he still preserves the old ways.

They went to bed at 8:00 p.m. since they continued to rise at 4:00 a.m. even after Grandpa retired from the railroad. They never understood folks who stayed up late and "wasted" kerosene. And they certainly never comprehended the modern idea of "burning" electric lights in every room of the house—at the same time.

It is interesting to realize the antique, "coal-oil" lamps my grandparents relied on were new inventions as recently as Great-Grandma Russell's young adulthood. The first kerosene, manufactured in the 1850s, was derived from coal. Even now, a few older mountain folks describe kerosene as "coal oil."

But when oil was discovered in 1859, the kerosene we know today was mass-produced as a petroleum byproduct. Being cheaper and cleaner than coal-based kerosene, it gained popularity in the 1860s as fuel for the newest kerosene lamps.

Imagine that our great-grandmothers thought a glass, kerosene lamp was the latest, fashionable addition for a mountain home. Such lamps seemed old-timey after electricity became available, but only four generations ago they were highly desired and quite up to date.

Kerosene lamps once glowed through the windows of thousands of homes in Appalachia, just as they did at Granny's house on Bear Mountain. I enjoyed the flickering shadows on the ten-foot ceilings, and I liked to follow Granny from room to room as she carried the lighted lamp. She stepped cautiously on the uneven wooden floor, so the glass globe didn't shake or wobble as she walked. And the little flame provided just enough illumination for us to avoid bumping into the furniture.

And as far as my grandparents were concerned, that was plenty of light. Granny didn't sew or read at night, anyway, though she often crocheted by lamplight as they listened to the battery radio. Crocheting was done by counting stitches, so semi-darkness was sufficient for her relaxing handiwork.

Since they ate an early supper, they seldom needed extra kitchen light. At nice restaurants, the fashionable ambiance for evening meals has always seemed amusing to me. Generally, the darker the dining room, the more expensive the food tends to be. Of course, I look forward to special occasions at favorite inns and resorts, but it's still fun to compare their lighting to Granny's house on Bear Mountain. Back then, a softly lit room didn't have "atmosphere." Instead, dim lights meant that electricity wasn't available so far back in the mountains. Thankfully, times have changed. Today we have the choice of bright, diffused, or indirect lighting at the touch of a button.

On Bear Mountain there weren't such options, so Granny regularly refilled lamps and trimmed the ribbon-like wicks. And she carefully washed the glass globes to remove any accumulated soot. Trimming a wick meant clipping off the crusty edge that had hardened from the heat; this helped the flame to burn evenly with less smoking. I liked to watch Granny perform these chores, especially when she polished the glass globes with a flour sack until they seemed to glisten.

The free fabric, saved from bags of flour, was readily available on a mountain farm. Those repurposed, cotton sacks were so soft they removed even the tiniest residue of smoke and soap streaks. Sparkling globes shined light much better, so Granny was quite "particular" about keeping them clean. She held them up in the sun to check for smudges, and I could sense her pride in how clear they looked.

As Granny buffed the globes, she often recalled a scary story about averting an explosion in a lamp years ago. Somehow, in the process of lighting it, she accidentally set the wick on fire deep inside the kerosene-filled, glass bowl.

She could hear the fire roaring and see flames leaping. Her first instinct was to toss the entire lamp outside into the yard.

When it hit the ground, the glass bowl cracked enough to release pressure, and the blaze burned itself out in the sand. She considered the loss of a good lamp a small sacrifice to save her own life and to prevent the house from catching fire. Granny certainly reacted bravely in that emergency, considering that the flaming lamp could have burst in her hands.

Despite such a scare, their lifelong reliance on "coal-oil" lamps had advantages. My grandparents never worried about ice storms disrupting electrical service. Their living room stayed warm, the battery radio still worked, pinto beans simmered on the kitchen woodstove for supper—and the "lights" remained on. Granny and Grandpa were content with "coal-oil" lamps as part of their good life on the farm. In fact, one of Granny's favorite sayings was, "We live right well on the mountain."

Hiking the new Bear Mountain road just before dark on winter afternoons, I have experienced nostalgic moments. Walking toward the home place, I enjoy lights shining through hillside trees from the neighboring housing development. As barren limbs sway in the distance, the lights appear to be close, dim, and flickering—as though they are glowing on the secluded plateau where the 1895 house once stood. For a moment, I am taken back to the days when "coal-oil" lamps glimmered through farmhouse windows. For many decades they provided nightlight on Granny's mountain, in the remote coves of Henderson County, and throughout Appalachia.

Ask the oldest person you know if they have memories of trimming wicks, or of winter evenings by lamplight. Younger folks can relate to the ambiance of softly lit rooms, even if they wouldn't understand the term "coal oil." Think about the days when kerosene lamps were common, and how recently modern electricity came to some areas of our mountains.

Mid-winter quilting was creative and necessary in the mountains

A cold, winter day was a good time to work on a patch-work quilt, Granny figured, and she used the down-time on the farm to try new patterns. While a pot of soup simmered on the back of the cookstove, I recall following her up the wide, wooden stairs to retrieve rag bags from the attic. Gusts of light snow swirled outside the kitchen windows as she began the enjoyable task of sorting and matching colors.

Ladies in her era used free, flour-sack material and scraps of outgrown or worn-out clothing to piece quilts. The term "recycling" was unfamiliar, but folks understood the concept. "Making do" with what they had was a way of life for thrifty farmwives. They rarely purchased new fabric for quilting, though Granny did when she needed solid colors for special patterns and for her prized, yo-yo bedspread.

Historically, American pioneer women valued cloth so highly that even tiny scraps were reused and not wasted. That's how they came to design quilt patterns that are still popular today: the single or double Dresden Plate, the Log Cabin, and various forms of the Star, Postage Stamp, and

Flower Basket patterns. These were happily shared with visiting kinfolk and neighbors. Early magazines and catalogs also featured patterns that could be ordered for as little as ten cents.

Granny was always excited to find a new design to personalize or duplicate during long, winter days. Each one-foot block of the pattern might require twenty (or fifty) tiny pieces. She searched in the bags, pulled out odd scraps, and arranged them into piles. Flour-sack fabric tended to have bright designs, so pale-blue strips from Grandpa's old work shirts added a softer, solid color. Separate stacks of predominately green, purple, blue, motley burgundies, and reds were heaped next to lavender and pinkish hues. They could be blended later, like the yellows, tans, and patterned browns with touches of orange that Granny favored.

Multicolored plaids, checks, variegated stripes, floral patterns (roses, daisies, and mixed bouquets) were used interchangeably according to availability. Although Granny artistically sorted scraps, country ladies didn't expect to color-coordinate a whole quilt. If they ran out of red plaid, they moved on to lavender stripes without being too concerned. As I watched with fascination, Granny set about cutting little triangles, circles, and rectangular shapes from the assortment of old clothes and wildly colored flour sacks.

Bits of cloth were soon scattered over the floor and the kitchen table, too. But Granny was in a creative mood, so the temporary "gaum" wasn't bothering her much. This was mildly amusing to me since Granny was ordinarily quite particular about not having things strewn over a room. Wisely, I didn't comment on the messy appearance of her creativity, and just enjoyed the moment with her.

By mid-afternoon, some of the foot-square blocks were beginning to take shape. Tomorrow, Granny could begin sewing little triangles together on the foot-powered Singer sewing machine. Eventually, all the blocks would be completed and ready to attach to each other. Each quilt required more pieces than I could count at age five, so the process was long and slow. Ladies had more patience back then for home-sewing, and they didn't expect to finish in a day, a week, or even a month.

Like Granny, they had to be cognizant of daily responsibilities. Grandpa still expected his lunch at 11 a.m. and his supper at 4 p.m. Although wintertime chores didn't include planting or harvesting, the cow needed to be milked, and butter churning couldn't wait too long. She had to gather a few eggs from the henhouse and carry water from the spring. Wood for the cookstove certainly didn't "tote" itself to the wood box, so fun quilt-making had to be scheduled between cooking, milking, churning, "toting" and carrying.

It is also interesting to remember that sewing wasn't done on Sunday during Granny's era. Although it was creative, quilting was still considered to be work, and mountain ladies like Granny observed their Sabbath as best they could in a farm situation. She knew the animals had to be fed and watered on Sunday, but craft projects could wait until Monday. And they always did.

During the Great Depression, Granny worked on her yo-yo bedspread for seven years, though she made other more-necessary quilts during that time. The red, green, blue, and white bedspread was extra special, so she didn't mind taking so long to finish such a creative project. In fact, she valued it so highly that the bedspread was never used overnight. Instead, she displayed it on the bed only when company was expected. After the "oohing and aahing" over such a handcrafted masterpiece, the prized bedspread was folded in the dresser drawer for safekeeping when visitors left.

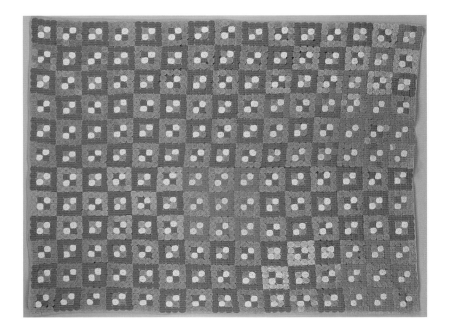

*17. Granny's yo-yo bedspread that she sewed for seven years
during the Great Depression*

Decades later, I continued to honor Granny's tradition of displaying the bedspread only if guests came. And in later years, I donated it to the Mountain Heritage Center Museum at Western Carolina University. Granny would be pleased that her seven-year, craft project is preserved for posterity and has never become tattered, soiled, worn-out, or discarded.

In addition to bedspreads, farm ladies like Granny worked diligently to create warm quilts that were used in the home. In cold, unheated rooms, several were necessary for each bed. There are true stories of snow blowing through the cracks of cabins and settling on bedcovers. The Bear Mountain house had been built more securely, but I still have fond memories of snuggling underneath Granny's colorful, patchwork quilts on blustery nights. However, quilt-making was a long process.

When Granny finally completed a quilt top, she "backed" it with yards of warm flannel purchased on a rare trip to town. For extra warmth, she stuffed quilts with thick, cotton batting from F. W. Woolworth's 5 and 10 Cent Store on Hendersonville's Main Street. Granny always considered these to be practical (vs. decorative) quilt-making expenditures.

Finally, she brought the long, wooden, quilting frame downstairs. Grandpa suspended it from the kitchen ceiling, and I remember the quilt-in-progress being attached at waist height. Then, they sat in split-bottomed, kitchen chairs and worked from the center of the rolled-up quilt.

Grandpa enjoyed sewing tiny stitches through all three layers. I wondered if he was just bored during retirement, but he seemed to like the change of routine. And he was surprisingly good at making little stitches that went 'round and 'round the design in every square. Granny appreciated his help since hand-quilting required days, and sometimes as long as two weeks.

Homemade quilts were needed in cold farmhouses, but in Granny's opinion, they could also be colorful, beautiful, and creative. Using recycled clothes, flour sacks, and some "bought" fabric, she designed quilts for sixty years (1910 to the early 1970s).

Granny would be glad that ladies today still enjoy quilting, but she would be amazed at modern quilt-making skills, supplies, and equipment. Computerized sewing machines and access to enough new fabric to design color-coordinated quilts would delight her. With such fun materials, she certainly wouldn't want to stop quilting long enough to milk the cow, to gather eggs, or to carry wood and water.

18. Among his antiques, Country Hawkins has an old-fashioned quilt. The design and assorted materials are similar to quilts that were pieced by older ladies during the Great Depression. They saved worn-out or out-grown clothing and flour-sack material for quilt making and rarely purchased new fabric.

Looking back, we can appreciate the diligence required for hand-quilting while ladies managed mountain farms without modern conveniences. Recall quilts in your family that were made for warmth, especially if they were sewed from rag-bag scraps or flour-sack fabric. And remember the comfort of snuggling beneath those thick, brightly colored quilts on snowy nights. Those warm, multicolored memories are to be treasured.

Farm folks rose early and cooked a hearty breakfast—even in winter

The big, red rooster crowed at 4 A.M. on Bear Mountain—even on the coldest mornings. If Grandpa hadn't already heard the 1912 mantle clock clang four times, he'd for sure hear the rooster. That was his cue to loudly announce, "Get up, Sal, its 4 o'clock!"

Nobody ever knew how he came up with such a nickname for Granny, but that's what he liked to call her. Perhaps it was another of their deep-rooted British traditions. Sal is a shortened version of Sally, but it was also used as a good-natured term of endearment for a special lady.

Granny usually went along with Grandpa's teasing—except at 4 o'clock on winter mornings. Then, she said she'd really like to sleep until 6 o'clock.

However, Grandpa continued to rise early, even after retiring from the railroad. He'd light the flickering kerosene lamp, and it cast a warm glow over the oilcloth-covered table while he built a fire. Soon, the wonderful aroma of coffee perking on the red-hot cookstove filled the house.

I would have to grow lots bigger to enjoy the good-smelling coffee the way Granny and Grandpa did. They liked it black and so hot they poured it from the cup into a saucer to sip it. This was a common practice in the mountains. The saucer under the cup wasn't there just for looks. It was used to drink the scalding coffee.

Still, I loved to smell it from the cold bedroom where I snuggled under Granny's thick, patchwork quilts. I'd heard Grandpa's early-morning announcement, of course, but as a young child, I wasn't brave enough to bounce out onto the icy, linoleum floor.

19. *Grits, bacon, and eggs were commonly cooked in ironware. Notice the brown eggs that were typical on mountain farms.*

By the time I finally did crawl out of the warm bed and dash to the kitchen, Granny had buttermilk biscuits ready to go in the oven. Grandpa had started the grits boiling and fried crisp slices of streaked fatback.

From years of practice, Granny stirred, browned, and thickened the sawmill gravy to perfection, adding just the right amount of rich milk. They used the more common mountain term for gravy which was "dough-sop." (Maybe it had been named because brown gravy was actually a form of thin dough that could be sopped with bread.)

Granny liked gravy by any name, but always said she had to have "a little sweetenin' with breakfast." She set out homemade butter and jam "ever mornin' of the week." She made enough to last all winter from the seasonal strawberries, cherries, and blackberries.

When it was almost time for the hot biscuits to come out, Grandpa scrambled a "passel" of eggs. They'd be just a tiny bit brown on the bottom the way he liked them. Fresh eggs from Granny's chickens were mighty tasty. (I enjoyed egg biscuits long before McDonald's made them famous.) Such a feast was enough to get anybody out of bed—even on the coldest morning!

Granny believed in the mountain tradition of big breakfasts. She always said, "It's where a'body gets their strength. If you don't eat a good breakfast, you'll give out a'fore you get anything done."

I could certainly go along with her country breakfasts, but one old-fashioned habit Granny had was beyond my childhood comprehension. Quite often, she drank a cup of plain hot water. That just seemed to be so very strange, but she assured me it was "good for a'body."

Since then, I've checked it out and found that some health advocates agree. Drinking hot water, it is believed, is very beneficial: It can help detoxify the body, purify the bloodstream, clear up congestion, calm the nervous system, and aid digestion. Granny somehow understood such benefits decades before modern researchers wrote about them.

By 6 o'clock, she dipped hot water from the cookstove reservoir and washed the dishes. She was "real partic'lar" about washing them immediately after each meal and often declared, "It just makes it harder to get'em clean later if you let'em set around."

Grandpa brought in an armload of heater-sized wood and "chunked up" the coals in the front room. It didn't take much to get a hot fire started, since the embers were usually red from the night before. Then, he rested in his rocking chair and turned on the battery radio for the early-morning news and weather.

Sometimes when I looked out the kitchen windows, there was a "skiff" of snow—just enough to make it look like winter. As daylight broke in the rose-colored sky across Hogback Mountain and reflected on the whiteness of the ground, Granny invited me to help feed the birds.

Wanting to instill a sense of appreciation and responsibility, she carefully explained, "God made the purty little birds, but He depends on us to help Him feed them in the cold wintertime." Thrilled to be needed, I trotted along beside her and crumbled leftover biscuits for God's pretty "snow-birds" as Granny called them.

Then, we'd come in and warm by the wood heater and listen to the rest of the news. She and Grandpa were always interested in hearing what President Truman said. Even with their limited understanding of politics, they avidly followed the current news stories of the day.

By the late 1940s, most people had electric radios, and TV was beginning to gain popularity. However, a battery-operated radio was still necessary on the secluded farm. It brought the outside world across the lofty Appalachian Mountains—all the way to my grandparents' living room!

Soon it was time for Granny to clean house and to carry fresh water from the spring. Grandpa liked his lunch on the table by 11 o'clock, and it was another of their big meals of the day. Without modern convenience foods, the midday meal was also prepared "from scratch."

Because mountain people lived so close to the land, family stories and memories tend to include numerous descriptions of food and its preparation. Farms were usually in isolated areas without modern amenities, so their day-to-day lives focused on how to survive, and even thrive, by creatively using available resources.

Mountain families spent many months of the year planting, hoeing, gathering, and preserving the bounty of the harvest, and all these were time-consuming processes. Back then, ladies didn't work outside the home, so their entire lives were centered on the farm.

In modern times we usually don't rise as early as 4 A.M. or prepare a country breakfast on a woodstove. For a quick meal, we can choose instant, prepackaged, frozen foods (or take-out). In Granny's era, electricity wasn't available—and many popular foods we take for granted hadn't been developed.

Times have changed, and life in the modern world certainly has its advantages. We can enjoy our choices, and still have an appreciation for the diligence, talents, and skills of our ancestors.

Think about the early-morning routine at an older relative's home when you visited. Recall the tantalizing aromas of bacon and coffee that filled the house—especially if breakfast was cooked on a woodstove on a cold morning.

Spring Stories

*20. Spring flowers are still glorious on Bear Mountain today.
In memory of Granny's thrift, we planted several colors.*

Mountain people foraged wild herbs for spring tonics

21. Mountain people started foraging for wild creasy greens just as the snows melted.

Mountain folks were firm believers in herbal teas and greens for natural spring tonics. Just as the last snows began melting, Granny searched for wild creasies growing in fields and along the edges of her garden. Since they were the earliest edible plants in the mountains, their fresh, leafy stems often poked through late-winter snows. The botanical name, *Barbaraea verna*, denotes that creasy greens are a mustard green like watercress, except the mountain variety doesn't grow in bogs. The name creasies came from "cress" of watercress, and the crisp greens could be added to salads. But Granny liked creasies simmered with fatback in an iron pot on the woodstove and served with crusty cornbread.

Country folks, who had subsisted all winter on canned and dried foods from last year's harvest, looked forward to fresh greens. Since creasies have twice as much vitamin A as broccoli, and three times as much vitamin C as oranges, no wonder Granny started watching for them to peek through the snow.

And she always declared that hot, Sassafras tea in early spring would "pearten a'body right up." By April she hiked through the forest and dug the aromatic roots of a young Sassafras tree (*Sassafras albidum*). Carrying a handful to the spout at the wash place, Granny carefully rinsed away woods dirt, and peeled the bark into strips. Mountain folks drank Sassafras tea as a spring tonic boiled with fresh, spring water. A fragrant, root-beer scent filled the entire house on those spring days. The resulting dark, red tea was considered quite healthful (although the FDA eventually banned the chemical *safrole*, found in Sassafras roots, from the U.S.).

Another of Granny's spring tonics was Spicebush tea, and she began gathering twigs as soon as leaves showed on the tree (*Lindera benzoin*). Twigs could be broken and steamed to make hot tea, somewhat lighter in color than Sassafras. Both were considered "blood builders" to cleanse the system of winter maladies. She served Spicebush tea with cornbread, and the flavors blended so well that a springtime meal sometimes consisted of tea and bread. In late spring, Granny again foraged for wild greens, this time for "Poke Salat," as she called it. Like other mountain terms, salat was a real word from the Old Country.

German settlers had introduced it, and in Appalachia, salat gradually came to mean cooked greens, while salad continued to describe raw greens. Pokeweed (*Phytolacca americana*) was edible when it was shorter than six inches, but only if the cook followed a complicated recipe passed down by Native Americans. The toxic plant grew to eight feet in summer—becoming even more poisonous.

Thankfully, Granny understood the old-time recipe, and safely prepared the spring delicacy (which had a high-vitamin content like creasies). Because kind Indians shared knowledge of living off the land, mountain folks, including my grandparents, looked forward to these annual fresh greens. One spring-tonic plant Granny and Grandpa would have enjoyed was ramps, which are wild leeks (*Allium tricoccum*). However, Bear Mountain is approximately 2,200 feet in elevation, and ramps prefer much-taller mountains closer to Mt. Mitchell.

Ramps combine the strongest flavors of both onions and garlic and contain vitamins A, B, C, E, and K, as well as Iron and minerals. They are extremely healthful and can be eaten raw—though the faint of heart prefer frying. Mountain folklore declares that one-room schools temporarily closed in springtime; teachers couldn't bear the combined bad breath of a roomful of mountain children who had been eating ramps. Still, I'm sure Granny would have foraged for such a nutritious plant.

WARNING: Do not consume wild vegetation without expert guidance. Mistaken identification or improper cooking can lead to serious illness or death.

Think about herbs that may have been gathered by your ancestors. And ask an older person to share spring-tonic stories they remember.

The year it snowed on Easter Sunday

I n addition to a special Easter service celebrating the Resurrection, teenage girls in the mountains tradition- ally looked forward to home-sewn Easter dresses. For teens interested in pretty clothes, the fashion-conscious 1950s were great years. Flared circle skirts, full-gathered skirts made from yards of fabric, suits with pencil-slim skirts, and sheath dresses were all stylish. The beautifully classic designs were dressy, crisply tailored, and uncluttered—to accentuate youthful waistlines.

Back then, Simplicity, Butterick, Vogue and McCall's were popular sewing patterns; each company's thick, coun- tertop catalog showed the most up-to-date spring trends. Fabric choices included rayon faille, rayon taffeta, cotton broadcloth, acetate, linen and linen-look rayon.

Surprisingly, polka dots, checks and stripes were featured along with colorful flower prints and classic solids. The Sears, Roebuck and Co. spring catalog arrived just after Christmas, so teenagers spent snowy, winter evenings admiring the lat- est colors and fashions. Cloth by the yard, accessories, or entire Easter outfits could be ordered and delivered via the U.S. Mail.

*22. On a sunnier Easter, Janie Mae wore a 1950s pink suit
with pink accessories, including a large, stylish hat.*

Girls compared catalog styles with those available in Hendersonville, and sometimes chose from both. That year, I shopped exclusively on Main Street—so I could be sure each purchase matched the others. After a long winter of tiresome, heavy coats and dark colors, it was fun to coordinate spring pastels. Pale pink, yellow, perhaps lavender, spring green or light blue were always exciting possibilities. But for some reason, white seemed better to me that fateful year. Easter reminded me of blue skies, sunshine, spring flowers, and robins hopping on new grass. I guess I hadn't considered that Easter would be in March that year, so I excitedly proceeded with plans for an all-white ensemble.

In those days, dress materials were sold by the yard at Mill Ends Store & Silk Shop on Main Street. After considering the many options, white linen was my fabric of choice, along with a beautiful Simplicity sheath-dress pattern. The Singer sewing machine whirred for days, and I was quite pleased with the finished handiwork. Annual Easter clothes typically included a new hat and white gloves, as well as a matching handbag and shoes. Girls and ladies still wore hats and gloves to church in the 1950s, especially on Easter.

Picture hats were fashionable, and specialty stores promoted millinery departments in anticipation of the spring season. That year Martin's Distinctive Styles Shop (also on Main) displayed the perfect white hat in their window, and I spotted it as soon as I crossed the street.

The wide brim caught my eye because it was completely covered with cascading layers of see-through nylon ruffles. At least six rows were tightly bunched together—like too many curtains on a curtain rod. Reminiscent of Scarlett O'Hara, it was definitely the hat for a would-be Southern belle in the 1950s.

Because of sewing the dress, the idea of splurging on the elaborately ruffled hat seemed more permissible. It was absolutely beautiful, I thought—and white looked good with the pointed-toe pumps I'd selected across the street at Holly Swofford's Shoe Store. Never mind that I had to practice wobbling around on three-inch, spike heels; they were the newest, slimmest style! Before Four Seasons Boulevard, Belk's and Penney's were on Main Street, and I shopped in both stores. They had the perfect white gloves and a delightful, white-linen clutch bag that coordinated with the dress.

23. Lightweight spring coats, called dusters, were popular in the 1950s. They could match or contrast with lovely spring dresses.

To add a little color to the all-white Easter attire, I did concede to a navy-blue, linen duster from Rayless Department Store (also on Main). These loose-fitting, unlined coats were designed with mid-length sleeves for spring—although I really didn't want to cover up my new, white dress.

Dusters were the latest fashion rage, and were shown in spring catalogs, on the fronts of sewing-pattern envelopes, and on well-dressed mannequins in store windows. The trendy coats could harmonize with a pastel Easter dress, or could contrast (just as beautifully) with the entire outfit.

Looking at 1950s catalogs now, I can't help but notice the similarities between ladies' knee-length housecoats and dusters. The loose, flowing silhouette and three-quarter-length sleeves were similar, except dusters for streetwear were made of thick, crisp linen. Thinner fabrics of soft nylon or cotton seersucker were preferred for robes and nightwear. Nevertheless, a fashionably dressed lady of the era considered a duster an added feature of her spring wardrobe.

It turned out to be an excellent idea The Year It Snowed on Easter Sunday. As a Henderson County native, I should have known to be wary of an early Easter. (Oh, the impetuousness of youth!) In North Carolina's mountains, daffodils and azalea blooms can be glazed with ice and snow in April. Weather in late March is often a mixture of winter and spring: sometimes warm, maybe cold, or even freezing. The Year of the White Easter Dress it snowed all day on Easter Sunday. At what should have been a golden dawn, thick clouds gathered over mountain peaks, and the snow started.

It spit, sputtered, blew about, and finally settled atop my ruffled hat—so I gingerly held it on with white-gloved fingers of one hand. The church parking lot was extremely slick, I discovered, as I balanced on three-inch heels in the fashionably tight dress (desperately clutching the white clutch bag). Fortunately, I remained upright without tumbling headfirst into the cemetery.

On that snowy Sunday, the amazing story of the empty tomb was retold in jubilant song and sermon. Full of Southern charm, the church folks highly complimented my all-white Easter costume. But as we were leaving, they candidly observed, "Goodness, Janie Mae, we can't see you for the snowflakes!" Unable to keep straight faces after that comment, they started giggling—so I did, too.

But when the snow melted, and spring finally arrived, I did enjoy the white dress and its matching accessories. It became a summertime favorite for several years. The extravagantly ruffled hat, purse, gloves, spindly heels (and the duster) easily coordinated with other outfits, so all was not lost.

However, since that ill-fated year, I've never worn another white Easter dress! Times have changed. These days, ladies and teenage girls don't look forward to new, spring clothes as much as we did in the 1950s. Hats and gloves for church have gone the way of seamed nylon stockings. Millinery departments have disappeared along with Sears-Roebuck catalogs. Most people wouldn't know a duster from an ordinary housecoat, and very few ladies still sew their own dresses.

Can you (or an older relative) remember shopping at Main Street department stores and wearing Easter hats, gloves, and stylish dusters? Think of a "disastrous" but very fashionable Easter ensemble in your younger days and share the hilarious story with someone.

Old-time radio and newspaper reports kept the nation informed

T he "new-fangled" battery radio brought news to secluded Bear Mountain along with President Franklin Roosevelt's Fireside Chats in the 1930s and 1940s. The first President to understand the power of radio communication, he endured himself to my grandparents and to millions of other Americans through those informal talks. Elected to four consecutive terms, the beloved leader offered hope during the Great Depression and courage in World War II.

Granny often talked about her memories of President Roosevelt's unexpected death April 12, 1945, at Warm Springs, GA. She was shocked, like most Americans, because his deteriorating health had been kept secret during wartime.

To provide continuous coverage honoring the late President, radio stations abruptly removed regular programming and commercials. Then, they hastily assembled microphones at train depots across four states. Radio networks made live broadcasts as the funeral train ceremoniously traveled 24 mph to Washington, D.C. (approximately 600 miles).

24. *The nation's grief at FDR's death is depicted at the Little White House
Museum. The original, full-page, LIFE magazine photo by Ed Clark
captured the tears of Navy CPO Graham Jackson. He was playing
"Going Home" as President Roosevelt's casket was being transported
from the Little White House, April 13, 1945.*

In their own way, ordinary folks paid tribute to the only
President some of them could remember. Through Georgia,
the Carolinas, and Virginia, over half a million people
lined railroad tracks. They patiently waited throughout
the day and into the night. Each wanted a glimpse of the
flag-draped coffin displayed in lighted windows of the last
train car.

*25. Larry and Janie Mae at the Little White House, Warm Springs,
GA, where President Franklin D. Roosevelt died April 12, 1945*

Ladies waved handkerchiefs, men placed hats over their hearts, and farmers knelt in nearby fields. Impromptu groups gathered at railroad crossings to sing Negro Spirituals and *Onward Christian Soldiers*. Sad, afraid, and uneasy, folks grieved for Franklin Roosevelt and worried whether a new President could finish winning the war. Newsmen of the day vividly described tear-stained faces in the crowds.

Then, the next broadcaster broke in as the funeral train passed through yet another crowded station on its north-ward trek. At times, announcers struggled with their own emotions as they interviewed weeping mourners. But their patched-together coverage provided minute-by-minute accounts of a national tragedy, and such efforts were an early version of modern, 24/7 news.

Completely engrossed in the drama of those live news-casts, Granny stayed close to the battery radio for hours. As she often recalled, "I didn't want to leave to carry water from the spring or to start supper. I just wanted to stay by the radio and listen as the train got to the next station." In rural Appalachia, she felt connected to "her" President through the miracle of a battery radio, a ground rod, and an antenna wire stretched to a locust post in the cornfield.

Because mountain folks like Granny were natural story-tellers, famous news events were discussed for decades. Eventually, I visited the Roosevelt Memorial at Warm Springs, GA. Throughout the tour of the Little White House, I thought of Granny's fascination with that news story back in 1945, and of her oft-repeated memories of FDR's death.

In 1941, my grandparents heard the first reports of Japan's surprise attack on Pearl Harbor. They always tuned in when President Roosevelt spoke, especially his famous speech as Congress declared war: "Yesterday, December 7th, 1941—a date which will live in infamy—the United States…was suddenly and deliberately attacked…." Later, they followed radio reports of President Truman's bombing of Japan. Like others with relatives serving in the long war, Granny and Grandpa were saddened, but relieved.

And I recollect the news being the "talk of the country" when President Truman fired General Douglas MacArthur. In mountain folks' expressed opinion, "Harry Truman showed more gumption than anybody in Washington!" But being apolitical, Granny and Grandpa supported WWII-hero, General Dwight Eisenhower in the 1952 election, because "he won the war against Germany."

Back in 1936, country people like my grandparents had been captivated by radio reports of the abdication of King Edward VIII. It was another well-known news event that I heard recounted into the 1950s. That the King of England would give up his throne for love was a compelling, true-life drama. That his choice was Wallis Simpson, a twice-di-vorced, 40-year-old American socialite, made it even more remarkable.

As a child I remember quotes from his abdication speech, sometimes from folks who recalled the actual broadcast: "... ou must believe me when I tell you that I have found it impossible to carry the heavy burden of responsibility...as King...without the help and support of the woman I love....

Hard-working mountain farmers marveled about the power of a love that compelled a king to renounce his throne. They openly wished that King Edward had the same freedom as ordinary men to choose a wife—and they felt richer by comparison.

Before radio, important news stories were gleaned from newspapers or magazines and shared by word of mouth; these were added to the repertoire of mountain storytellers for decades to come. Well into the 1950s, I heard discussions about the 1912 sinking of the Titanic—the ship designed to be unsinkable. The ill-fated Titanic went to the bottom of the Atlantic on its maiden voyage, and over 1,500 lives were lost.

Practical country folks were of the opinion the builders "shoulda knowed" that any ship could sink. And they "shorely oughta knowed to take plenty of lifeboats when they started across that deep water."

During my childhood, the dramatic story made frequent references to Titanic's orchestra. Although that version has been questioned in recent years, it was once widely reported. Brave musicians were said to have stopped performing scheduled songs and switched to *Nearer My God to Thee*. Even as the deck sloped toward the ocean, they continued playing. Finally, one by one, heroic band members and their instruments were swallowed by icy waves.

When the tragedy was so theatrically repeated to me, folks were glad that some good came from it. Afterward, oceangoing vessels were required to provide lifeboats for all passengers.

In the 1950s, I also recall troubling accounts of the Lusitania's sinking in 1915. The German-submarine attack, that killed over 100 American civilians, brought European conflicts closer home. Despite Woodrow Wilson's campaign slogan, "He Has Kept Us Out of War," the President finally asked Congress to declare war in 1917.

And decades later, I remember mountain folks proudly bragging about "their" hero. During that First World War, Sgt. Alvin York from nearby Tennessee, received the Medal of Honor for battlefield bravery in capturing 132 German soldiers. One of Granny's brothers served in the Great War, and he sent her a magazine about Sgt. York. She treasured it for 60 years and hand-sewed the pages when they became tattered. Later, I donated the rare magazine to a York memorial school in Tennessee, where it is displayed for posterity.

Before television and the internet began inundating us with 24-hour coverage, old-time radio, newspaper, and magazine reports received undivided attention. Great news events, told and retold by mountain storytellers, became legends that were passed to the next generations. Like Granny's memories, they never seemed to grow old. Spectacular world events provided dinnertime and front-porch conversation for years to come. News stories were debated at country stores and recounted around firesides on winter nights.

26. A page from Granny's treasured World War I magazine shows Sgt. York being greeted by his mother upon his safe return as a national hero.

Think of historic events you heard discussed as a child. Would some of them have happened before television? Recall natural storytellers in your family or neighborhood who kept news reports alive long after the actual occurrences.

Some of our current news will be remembered and retold, even though Prince Harry's leaving the Royal Family isn't quite as dramatic as his Great-Great Uncle's abdication. But it is almost certain that future generations will hear stories about the 2020 Coronavirus pandemic.

May meant early garden vegetables—and a whole week at Granny's

I n the late 1940s and early 1950s, elementary school ended the last week of May. The timing was perfect since Granny's first garden vegetables were coming in. I looked forward to her old-timey cooking and to leisurely days of summer on Bear Mountain. Visiting their secluded farm after the busy school year—and getting to stay a whole week—was pure joy and delight.

Wildflowers along the trail added to the beauty of the mile-long hike from the nearest highway. The entire forest was leafing out with new, spring growth, and Mountain Laurels were heavy with pink and white blossoms. After I crossed a gurgling stream and climbed the spring-trail hill, Granny's prized flower garden came into view. Carefully tended varieties bloomed in glorious color from early spring throughout the summer.

Their tin-roofed farmhouse on the scenic, natural ridge was quite modern—back in 1895. Granny recalled that the Bear Mountain house had been the "talk of the country" when it was being built. She remembered stories from her own childhood about the history of the house, and I never tired of hearing them.

Unlike one-room, log cabins of the era, it had been designed with interior rooms (including a kitchen). "Folks marveled," Granny said, "about having doors inside the house—as well as on the outside." She always mentioned that the kitchen itself was an up-to-date feature in the 1800s. Because of the danger of fire, mountain folks often built kitchens in separate log structures some distance from the house.

Granny talked about the real glass windows (instead of more-common wooden shutters) in every room. "Most local folks couldn't have afforded the Bear Mountain house when it was first built," she said, "since it was bigger than mountain cabins, and was made of boards instead of logs."

Back then, it was in a great location: "Farmers needed to be close to the stagecoach road," Granny explained. Although the railroad arrived in Hendersonville in 1879, wagons, carts, and stagecoaches still rumbled through the mountains for a couple of decades. However, by the early 1900s, the popularity of freight and passenger trains gradually ended the era of horse-drawn conveyances.

By 1917, when Granny and Grandpa first purchased the farm, the nearby stagecoach road was almost impassable except as a walking trail. Without an access road, the once-fine house with real glass windows and interior doors depreciated in value. Then, it became more affordable to a working man like Grandpa. Modern roads (with modern conveniences) just didn't go to Bear Mountain—and it was that way for a long, long time.

However, during those enjoyable summers, I looked forward to hiking a mile through the forest to visit my grandparents. They lived quite contentedly on the secluded farm where time seemed to linger a century behind. Their quaint kerosene lamps and wood cookstove just added to the adventure, especially since I knew the history of their picturesque homestead.

I was enthralled with the storybook beauty of the peaceful mountain, the 1895 house, its well-kept yard, and pretty flower garden. For a whole week, I shared my grandparents' enjoyment and pleasure in the warm days that brought the first garden vegetables.

As Granny always said, "We live right well on the mountain," and the early harvest from the garden proved her point. Warmed by the sun and dampened by misty fog, spring lettuce grew tall, green, leafy, and so tender. Granny and Grandpa were mighty partial to this vitamin-rich delicacy that was available just once a year, and they especially enjoyed it with early spring onions.

On a brisk May morning with dew sparkle still on the garden, Granny went to the lettuce patch and gathered a bucketful. After pulling several bunches of early onions, she toted the fresh greens to the spring branch.

Without the modern convenience of running water in her home, it was easier to take the vegetables down the hill and wash them in the flowing stream. Carrying extra buckets of water up the steep spring trail just to wash vegetables would have been difficult and time consuming, as well.

Granny "looked" the lettuce really well as she held each individual leaf under the spout in the splashing, cold water. Then, to be sure it was clean, she dropped it into the tub underneath the spout to swish around, carefully washing away any remaining dirt and possible garden bugs. The already tender lettuce plumped up crisp and cold from its icy, spring-water bath. The spindly, green onions were washed after the lettuce was removed from the tub, since more garden dirt tended to cling to them.

After carrying the spring delicacies up the trail to the house, Granny built a fire in the wood cookstove. Now, she was ready to bake a "pone" of cornbread in a heavy iron skillet and fry thick slices of streaked fatback bacon. Her special culinary method, developed over the years, was to fry the fatback very slowly, turning each piece frequently until it became crisp and golden brown. She removed it from the pan but continued to keep the grease hot on the back of the stove.

27. Fresh lettuce and spring onions served with streaked fatback bacon, cornbread and buttermilk are reminiscent of Granny and Grandpa's favorite spring-time meal.

Next, she chopped the lettuce and long green onions together and piled heaps onto each plate along with slices of the browned bacon. Crusty cornbread, thick and hot, was flipped onto an oversize platter in the middle of the table.

At exactly 11:00 a.m. when Grandpa was seated, she brought the frying pan of hot grease and drizzled some over the lettuce and onions in each plate. It made a sizzling, frying sound as it wilted the crisp lettuce. A tall glass of country buttermilk set off this tasty, spring meal.

They enjoyed fresh lettuce and onions nearly every day for a couple of weeks, often corresponding with my week-long visit. Then the summer sun toughened the lettuce, and the green onions matured. They knew they'd have to wait until next year for this wonderful treat—and they were already looking forward to it.

It took a while to appreciate Granny's next garden vegetable, because the only green peas I'd ever eaten came from a can. She had planted English peas early, so they were ready just as the lettuce harvest ended. Her method of steaming entire pea pods (after stringing them) was different, but I learned to like the fresh taste. The hulls were as tender as the peas, I soon discovered.

As with other farm foods, Granny had developed her own special recipe: quick steaming the plump pods with a little water, lots of butter, and just a "pinch" of salt. Some hulls burst from the steam, while others stayed intact. I enjoyed separating them on my plate before hungrily devouring the whole pods first.

Such were the simple, summertime pleasures on Bear Mountain in the early 1950s. Think about idyllic childhood summers, especially if you enjoyed serenity, beauty—and fresh vegetables—on a country farm.

Share stories about the history of your ancestors' home place with younger generations. We only have memories of such old-fashioned houses nowadays—but they can be lasting memories.

Granny practiced "social distancing" on Bear Mountain

Since mid-March 2020, when Coronavirus changed our busy lifestyles, I have thought a lot about Granny's daily life. Now, Larry and I are quarantined on beautiful Bear Mountain where she lived. The spring flowers she planted so long ago are blooming, and wild irises, mountain magnolia, laurel, and native azaleas grace her mountain as they always did. She enjoyed such natural beauty, and we do, too.

Although the term "social distancing" wasn't known during Granny's lifetime, she certainly stayed away from other people. On secluded Bear Mountain she was indeed quarantined. That was a word folks were familiar with since quarantines had been required in populated areas during outbreaks of infectious diseases like diphtheria and tuberculosis.

Perhaps our socially distanced lifestyle isn't as satisfying as hers, but it is easy to temporarily forget the outside world while relishing the beauty and serenity of Bear Mountain. With modern conveniences, we have more time than Granny did to stroll the mountain trails and appreciate seasonal wildflowers. When she hiked through this beauty, she was carrying water buckets, five gallons at a time, stopping at the resting root halfway up the trail. Multiple daily trips to the spring were required to operate the household. Our well, powered by electricity, pumps hundreds of gallons directly into the house. She gathered, split, and stacked firewood for the cookstove. We can microwave food almost instantly (an unimagined convenience during her lifetime).

A springtime view of Granny and Grandpa's home, built on Bear Mountain in 1895. The oil painting by Zirconia folk artist, the late Mrs. Myrtle Pace, was donated to the Mountain Heritage Center Museum, Western Carolina University.

However, trees recently fell across local power lines and cut off our electricity for 40 hours. Then, the shortcomings of modern living became obvious. Our mandated quarantine on beautiful Bear Mountain suddenly became very inconvenient. Without an online newspaper or television, news from the outside world was difficult to obtain. But I remember that Granny and Grandpa would listen to broadcasts from faraway places every night on their old-fashioned, battery radio.

Without electricity, we went to bed at dark like they did, but limited to modern, bottled water, we temporarily postponed laundry. Granny regularly washed clothes using a creek-side battling block with water heated in the iron washpot. However, I chose to wait 40 hours so I could simply push buttons on my automatic washer. Few of us nowadays could manage washpot laundry. When electrical service is disrupted, we can certainly appreciate our strong family heritage. We are descended from hearty, hard-working forebears.

Instead of living like Granny during the power outage, we (modern wimps) resorted to disposable Styrofoam dishes at home, drive-through restaurants for quick meals, and convenience-store newspapers and cappuccino. Such options were non-existent during Granny's lifetime on Bear Mountain.

Before anybody thought of restaurants with pick-up windows, she served hot food at the kitchen table. Biscuits came from the wood-fired oven, and breakfast eggs from the henhouse, rather than in drive-through wrappers. Coffee percolated on the woodstove instead of being squirted, already sweetened, from a machine. Times have certainly changed.

It is noteworthy that Granny's daily lifestyle (without electricity) exemplified both social distancing and quarantining without her being aware of either. For weeks at a time, the only person she would see was Grandpa when he came home from work on the railroad. It never occurred to her to think this was unusual, lonely, or challenging on their mountain.

The nearest neighbors were a mile away, so visits were infrequent; they were busy with farm chores, as well. Having "company" on Sunday afternoon was unusual and quite special. Since going to Hendersonville was an all-day trip, Granny went maybe three or four times a year. Grandpa picked up mail and groceries on his way home from work, so she rarely needed to walk two miles to the Zirconia Post Office and Maybin's Grocery.

She didn't miss these excursions because she didn't have time for them, anyway. Her daily chores involved rising at 4 a.m. and preparing Grandpa's breakfast on the wood cookstove by the light of an oil lamp. By daylight, in the spring, summer, and fall, Granny was in the fields, planting, hoeing, and gathering farm crops. The pigs and chickens had to be fed, the cow milked, and more water "toted" from the spring. Butter needed to be churned, too, so mornings flew by. In mid-afternoons she carried wood from the woodshed and started cooking Grandpa's supper.

There were no instant, frozen, or prepared foods back then, so she made everything from scratch, peeling, chopping, and mixing by hand. Even a simple meal of crusty cornbread crumbled into steaming vegetable soup, served with a glass of buttermilk, and maybe a fresh-fruit cobbler, required several hours of preparation. But it certainly was tasty when they were tired from a long day's work, and I have fond memories of Granny's homestyle cooking.

After washing dishes and listening to news on the battery radio, my grandparents went to bed by 8 p.m. Nights seemed short; they knew the wind-up mantle clock would soon clang four times. Then, the early-morning routine would be repeated. Granny really didn't have time to think about shopping, going places, or leaving the mountain. Social distancing was just a consequence of a country lifestyle, and it seemed so natural she didn't feel isolated, lonesome, or quarantined at all. She didn't take "cabin fever," because she was busy putting food on the table.

Like our new-normal procedure, I remember that Granny also wore a mask and gloves—when she "robbed" honey from the beehives. On those occasions, she donned a special hat with a screened mask. It was secured with a tight draw-string around her neck with coverings for her shoulders. She wore two pairs of Grandpa's overalls, a couple of shirts, and a long coat. Then, she put on two pairs of gloves. At age five, I remember thinking her outfit was rather comical. But the bee stingers couldn't penetrate so many layers, and with a thicker mask, I'm sure today's Coronavirus couldn't have, either.

Granny's lifestyle served her well during the Great Depression when unemployment remained above 25 percent far longer than today's worst predictions. None of us wants to return to subsistence farming, but in light of the current situation, we can respect the advantages of the way our grandparents lived.

A temporary power outage, coupled with the ongoing shutdown, suggests that modern-day lifestyles aren't as sustainable as we wish they were. During such unusual times, we can be thankful that the food-supply chain has worked as well as it has. But empty grocery-store shelves due to inter-ruptions in food shipments make us long for Granny's garden and over-flowing can house.

With more time at home, many of us are trying our hand at vegetable gardening. It is thought-provoking to remember that just a few generations ago, mountain people grew most of their food. There were no telephones, televisions, computers, electricity, microwaves, washing machines, dish-washers, or vacuum cleaners, and very few roads or auto-mobiles. Only those with the luxury of a battery radio heard news broadcasts on a regular basis.

Still, my grandparents were content with a simple life on a secluded farm, even during the times Grandpa was laid off work. I am reminded that Granny's favorite saying during those hard years was, "We live right well on the mountain." Hopefully, we can emulate her spirit of gratitude as we quarantine and remain socially distant from the lives we have known.

Count your own blessings during these uncertain days, and recall memories of your grandparents' strengths and talents, especially during the Great Depression. Can you remember their stories of other quarantines because of contagious diseases?

Granny's flowers still bloom at the old home place

Although no one has lived at the Bear Mountain home place since 1956, Granny's Irises, daffodils, and day lilies still bloom every spring. They are an ongoing testament to her care and to her appreciation of beauty.

It was always amusing to observe how particular Granny was about her flower garden, especially since chickens roamed freely in the yard. It was common practice to open the chicken-house door every morning since farm chickens pecked and scratched for a substantial amount of their food. (Free-range chickens are not just a modern concept; country folks like Granny and Grandpa always raised poultry that way.)

To protect her special flowers, Granny had built a sturdy, picket fence around the flower garden. If one of the bolder chickens managed to flutter overtop that barrier, she wouldn't hesitate to use the chopping ax on its spindly neck.

Granny was usually a mild-mannered lady, but ruining her flowers was an unpardonable offence. That chicken immediately became a candidate for Sunday dinner—if she was in a notion of waiting that long. Otherwise, it could be on the menu the same day.

A hiker might have thought Granny's carefully tended flower garden was an unexpected sight at the edge of the isolated forest. Over the decades she had collected an assortment of perennials that bloomed every year. Annual varieties that naturally reseeded kept the flower garden bright all summer, as well.

Among the first signs of spring, Creeping Phlox (known as Thrift) bloomed, all fluffy, pink, and pretty. I remember masses of tiny flowers cascading down the rock wall that Granny had designed and laid. The stones she gathered from the hillside are still in place, though my attempts at replanting Thrift there haven't been nearly as successful.

28. Granny's flowers still bloom at the old home place. Notice that the "high steps" mentioned in this story remain decades after the house was torn down.

Beginning in early spring, Granny enjoyed bright-yellow daffodils in both the front and back yards. Along with her blue Iris, and day lilies, they are still blooming and spreading—more than sixty years later.

As the flowering season progressed, her favorites included snap dragons, Forget-me-nots, dahlias, lilies, tall Phlox, gladiolas, bleeding hearts, marigolds, and her special Sweet William.

Officially known as *Dianthus barbutus*, Sweet William was unusually beautiful with mixed maroon, pink, and white hues in each tiny petal. Crowded together, the variegated designs formed thick blooms on foot-tall stems, and the effect was quite pleasing to the eye.

Old-fashioned foxglove plants added their showy spikes to the harmonious jumble of color, too. Ranging from white to pink to dark rose on the same stem, this flowering native of the British Isles sometimes grew several feet tall. Back then, who would have thought the poisonous *Digitalis purpurea* would become a source of modern-day heart medication?

During my entire childhood, I never knew of Granny purchasing flowers because of the old-time custom of neighborly sharing. Country folks never let a visiting lady leave without a shrubbery cutting, a handful of seeds, or some freshly dug bulbs.

Such generosity was the height of Southern hospitality, and gifted plants in Granny's yard bloomed from spring through fall. And she certainly returned that same consideration to her own guests. Living on secluded Bear Mountain, Granny was thrilled to have company and to share her flowers.

After enjoying her good, country cooking, it was customary for ladies to walk outside and admire the over-flowing flower garden. Granny was delighted to offer, "Take some of these flower seeds. They'll come up next year. I'll get a poke for you to carry them home in, and I'll give you some of these snowball cuttings, too. Just root them in the creek for a while."

Visitors always marveled at Granny's snowball bushes; they seemed to grow taller and fuller every year. She had planted them around the edges of the yard, and the backdrop of white against the forest was stunning. However, she also enjoyed experimenting.

She had tried the new Kool-Aid that became popular in the early 1950s. Although she didn't have ice on Bear Mountain, the instant drink was quite tasty mixed with sugar and cold, spring water.

One summer day Granny came up with an idea: "What if I make a pitcher of grape Kool-Aid a little stronger than usual and pour it under a white snowball bush in the front yard?" Since I was just eight years old, I was game to try any of her adventurous experiments.

She laughed and wondered aloud as we doused the roots with the dark liquid, "Do you reckon it'll turn the snowballs blue next summer?"

And, sure enough, it did!

For about three seasons, that bush stood out from all the others in the yard with its bright, blue flowers. After that, Granny slowed down on her own Kool-Aid consumption, declaring, "Gracious! Think what it's doin' to our stomachs if it dyed the snowballs so bright and purty like that!"

In recent years, I have planted several blue hydrangeas on Bear Mountain in memory of Granny's fun experiment. Blue is a popular color nowadays. But no one had heard of it when she emptied that pitcher of grape Kool-Aid underneath her white-flowering bush. Perhaps she came up with that idea just to entertain me, but I thought it was great fun.

Granny also invited me to sit on the "high steps" (as they called them) after our early 4 o'clock supper. She said if we watched carefully we could actually see her treasured Four O'clock shrub begin to bloom.

Originally from Peru, the flowering bush, known as Marvel of the Night or *Mirabilis jalapa*, really does bloom between 4 p.m. and 6 p.m. Since they don't like the heat of the day, the colorful flowers open in late-afternoon coolness. Then, they bloom all night and close again in the bright, morning sun.

To me, it was magical to watch for the dark-red blooms to open. Granny pointed out the ones she saw, as well, and I thought each new flower was quite amazing.

Looking back, I think of the serenity and simplicity of life on Bear Mountain. It is unlikely in today's fast-paced, technological world that a grandparent and child would enjoy sitting on the steps waiting for flower buds to open. Time seemed to move more slowly in those days, especially at Granny and Grandpa's remote home place.

The one exception to my grandparents purchasing an ornamental tree was Grandpa's favorite pink dogwood. Though the woods were full of white dogwoods, he excitedly looked forward to those delicate, pink blooms every spring. Maybe the tree realized its specialness, because it continued to flower for fifty years after his passing. Then, it too, died, after decades of blossoming alone in a forest of white dogwoods. In recent years, we planted another pink dogwood, but somehow, it has never seemed happy on the mountain.

The other trees in the forest are taller now. The white dogwoods, mountain laurels, and wild azaleas continue to burst with color every spring. And Granny's special flowers still bloom in her yard, though free-range chickens no longer endanger their tender petals.

Think of old-fashioned flowers that grew at your older relatives' home places. Are some varieties still available today? Maybe you have some of them to enjoy this season.

When driving past an older home, especially if no one lives there, notice any colorful flowers that still bloom in the yard. Think about the lady who planted them so long ago and appreciate the beauty she continues to share with us today.

Socks were worn
with high-heeled shoes

During the Great Depression and World War II, it was common for mountain ladies to wear socks with high-heeled shoes. Old family photographs preserve this fashion statement from that era.

There were many reasons for this trend, and all were quite practical. The financial effects of the Great Depression were very real; ladies just couldn't afford expensive silk stockings. In those days, such luxuries could cost as much as $1.00 a pair if they were available. This amount could represent a third of some working girls' weekly paycheck (for those fortunate enough to have jobs).

Beyond cost concerns, many women, including my mother and her cousin, still lived in remote areas. Parts of Henderson County were accessible only by footpaths for generations, and Bear Mountain didn't have a road until 1975. Walking steep trails wearing delicate, easily snagged stockings would not have been practical even if a lady could afford them.

Nylon stockings were just coming onto the scene when World War II began. The military needed the newly invented synthetic material for ropes, and they used silk for parachutes. Such valuable resources couldn't be wasted just so ladies could look pretty, and the people agreed.

29. Double-first cousins, Misses Bess Russell (left) and Virgie Jane Russell pose with flowering Mountain Laurel (Kalmia latifolia) on Bear Mountain. Springtime weather was suitable for pretty, short-sleeved dresses and matching socks worn with high-heeled shoes. The lovely photograph was hand-tinted by Virgie since black-and-white film was the only choice in the late 1930s.

During wartime as many as 70 percent of Americans believed the government should ask for even more personal sacrifices from the folks at home. Rationing and recycling were willingly taught and practiced in daily life to help win a worldwide, two-front war.

Out of patriotism and practicality, mountain ladies were quite content wearing socks with both casual and high-heeled shoes. Besides, they could match the colors with their dresses, which they couldn't have done with fancy silk stockings, anyway.

It is interesting that this old-time fashion trend, necessitated by the effects of the Great Depression and World War II, has come around again. Trend-setting young ladies nowadays consider wearing socks with high heels to be fashion-forward, comfortable, elegant, and sophisticated. The combination is thought to create the essence of antiquity while combining it with polished, casual modernity.

Fashion-conscious young (and young-at-heart) ladies can make socks with heels the statement piece of their outfits, adding an element of excitement to otherwise ordinary clothing combinations. They consider this "new" trend a way of revealing their bold personalities. In fact, the innovative style has come into vogue partly because colorful socks can be matched with dresses and skirts (like other ladies discovered so long ago).

The concept of fashion comes and goes and comes again—in totally different eras—for totally different reasons. Combinations that once looked odd and strange may not seem so dated and old-fashioned in a new century.

It might be interesting to review old family photographs from the 1930s and 1940s. Look for socks worn with high heels, and recall stories you may have heard about practical fashions from that era. Make notes about your memories so you can share them with younger generations, since they may actually be dressed in similar combinations. Wearing socks with high-heeled shoes is not a wartime necessity today. Instead, the bold style is trendy, daring—and fashion-forward.

Summer Stories

30. Granny and Janie Mae on Bear Mountain in 1946

Summertime on Bear Mountain brought warm sun, gentle breezes, short-sleeved dresses, and outdoor activity.

Frog Level was a real place

31. Fruit stands like this one were common in the South during the 1940s and 1950s. Notice long, outdoor clotheslines displaying colorful chenille bedspreads for sale.

A gurgling creek flowed beside U.S. Highway 25 through the narrow valley between Tuxedo and Zirconia in southern Henderson County. When numerous frogs hopped onto the pavement, pickup trucks and "tourister" cars smashed scores of them: Squish! Splat! Crunch! So, the locals jokingly named the area Frog Level.

Despite the unsavoury label, Frog Level was quite a charming place, especially when it blossomed with tourist businesses every summer. In the late 1940s and early 1950s, beach travelers returning to northern states like Michigan and Ohio preferred the well-known U.S. Highway 25.

Competing shops on both sides of the highway displayed multi-coloured chenille bedspreads on long clotheslines. Red, yellow, purple, orange, blue or pink flower patterns were interwoven with bright-green leaf designs. Summer breezes floating down the valley danced and frolicked with the bedspreads, charming tourists as they drove around the Lake Summit curve.

They admired long outside tables loaded with fresh peaches, watermelons, cantaloupes, tomatoes, squash, and green peppers. Displays of Native American dolls and bow-and-arrow sets were enticing to children – especially when one enterprising shop owner (wearing bright feathered regalia) war-whooped through the parking lot and posed for "Indian" pictures.

For snacks, each shop featured glass-bottled Coca-Colas, Lance peanuts, R.C. Colas, moon pies and candy bars. Dozens of triangular-shaped felt pennants, emblazoned with red or blue *Great Smoky Mountains* logos, brightened the pine-panelled shop walls.

Out front, multi-colored pinwheels on sticks whirled in the wind with the bedspreads, enhancing the roadside appeal. In this cacophony of sight, sound and color, dozens of cement chickens, ducks, and deer stood at attention facing the highway. Yard art was popular, but if tourists didn't want to overload their cars, they could opt for scenic postcards or "genuine" corncob pipes.

Unfortunately, Frog Level's colorful tourist shops disappeared when the I-26 connecting artery came through the valley. Admittedly, I enjoy driving on the new highway, but I always imagine dozens of flowery, old-fashioned chenille bedspreads blowing in the breezes – when I venture off the modern freeway onto the old, two-lane road.

I-26 was predicted during the Great Depression

32. At the I-26 connecting highway's Exit 5 near Tuxedo, tall bridges and busy highways now cross over Frog Level – just as Uncle Mont predicted.

During the Great Depression, local people could not imagine that prosperity would ever come to the mountains again. Hard times were surely here to stay.

At least, that's the way it seemed to most folks.

However, Uncle Mont Jones, the Zirconia, NC, postmaster, had a different world view. He foresaw an economy so prosperous that U.S. Highway 25 would no longer be sufficient. In those days, north-bound traffic from Greenville, SC, came through Tuxedo and Zirconia. It continued to Flat Rock and downtown Hendersonville on the way to Asheville. Uncle Mont predicted a time when thousands of daily vehicles would overwhelm the existing two-lane highway.

33. Great-Uncle Mont's full name was
Montraville Lafayette Jones, Sr. (1877-1952)

He told people he'd been figuring how the government could possibly manage to get a big, wide highway through the small, Tuxedo community. The only way he could see it happening would be to bring the new road from the east. That meant it would pave over the area locally known as

Frog Level and continue across the forested mountain above Tuxedo to South Carolina. Then, traffic from Atlanta could be connected through Greenville into Asheville, toward Tennessee to the north and west, and into Winston-Salem, Durham, and Raleigh to the east.

Such an idea was so ludicrous that folks laughed in his face!

They tried to point out that after the summer residents left, only an occasional car or truck used the two-lane highway. Most country people walked everywhere they went and couldn't afford to drive, even if they'd bought a car before the Great Depression. In this era of "Hoover Buggies" country folk sometimes hitched mules to their Model-A Fords. This made a statement about their opinion of the economy—and provided a creative and quite comfortable mode of transportation.

But Uncle Mont was undeterred by their derision, their laughter, or their guffaws.

He admitted the new road probably wouldn't happen during his lifetime, but said, "Mark my words, the widest highway anybody's ever seen will come from the east and go right through Frog Level."

He was correct on all counts. After World War II, the economy did recover with unheard-of prosperity. Although Uncle Mont passed away in 1952, his ideas were on target.

Today, traffic swarms the wide I-26 connecting highway—that came from the east. Thousands of cars and trucks from Atlanta and Greenville cross the tall bridges—constructed over the area formerly known as Frog Level. Transport trucks, tourist cars, as well as local vehicles, now travel on four lanes to Asheville, toward Tennessee to the north and west, and into Winston-Salem, Durham, and Raleigh to the east. As this book goes to print, construction is under way to widen I-26 to six lanes.

The Frog Level tourist shops on two-lane U.S. Hwy. 25 have given way to an astounding level of growth. And Uncle Mont knew it before anyone else.

Think about old-time visionaries you may have known who, like Uncle Mont, foresaw great changes that eventually came to pass.

Young folks with cars were popular during the Great Depression, just before World War II

During the difficult years of the Great Depression, the national unemployment rate was sometimes over 25 percent. In North Carolina's mountains, it was probably higher, so a lot of people didn't have the luxury of driving. Most folks, young and old, walked everywhere they went, even if it was several miles.

There were stories of those with automobiles from better times hooking mules to the vehicles and riding in comfort without gasoline. Such make-do forms of transportation were jokingly referred to as "Hoover Mobiles" because President Hoover was widely blamed for the Great Depression.

During those tough times, building contractors relied on small jobs and looked for bargain materials. In some Southern states, an unusual source was license-plate suppliers. Thousands of metal license plates could not be sold for the intended purpose because folks couldn't afford to drive. Builders purchased truckloads of outdated, new tags at the low price of two for one penny (200 for $1.00). Then, they hauled them to job sites and cleverly repurposed the license plates as roofing shingles. Such "Hoover roofs" were economical for homeowners, and they lasted longer than standard roofs.

But the hard times were unrelenting. Businesses were closing, banks were failing, and farmers were facing foreclosure. The overwhelming election of 1932 delivered 42 of the 48 states (including North Carolina) to Franklin Roosevelt. He started to reverse the economic downturn; but recovery was slow, especially on mountain farms.

In the late 1930s, used cars sold for as much as $500.00, and automobile-operating expenses could be considerable. In addition to license plates, oil, and repairs, gasoline cost perhaps 19 cents per gallon. About 15 miles per gallon was standard, and even the best Depression-era tires didn't last long. Scraps of blown-out tires were commonplace along mountain roadside.

In the distressed economy, young men who were successful enough to drive their own cars never lacked for friends. They became instantly eligible and could attract almost any girl in the country. Those girls also had other friends with boyfriends. Then, some younger cousins would join the group. Gathering a carload of young people to enjoy a Sunday-afternoon drive was easy when "riding somewhere" was a real treat.

Still, the international news was troubling. Despite U.S. avoidance of overseas entanglements, President Roosevelt began strengthening the military for self-defense. The rumbles of European wars were coming closer with German U-boats trolling the Atlantic. However, Japanese capabilities were grossly underestimated. The far-off Empire of Japan was viewed as problematic, rather than threatening. But the malicious Pearl Harbor attack was secretly being planned, and it would happen on December 7, 1941.

34. *Janie Mae's mother, Miss Virgie Jane Russell (seated at the left on the running board) is shown some years before marriage and motherhood. The car is a 1931 Model-A Ford Deluxe Coupe, the windshield is open from the bottom for added summertime ventilation, and a brick has been placed at the back wheel to prevent the car from rolling down the mountainside. Notice the cornfield in the background.*

In the meantime, young people were focused on good times they could enjoy now. Back then, car seats were designed like upholstered benches, so as many folks as possible rode along for the trip. Before modern seatbelts and individual seats, teenagers enjoyed seeing how many friends could fit into their cars.

Imagine traveling 35 mph on U.S. Hwy. 25 toward Hendersonville (and beyond) with a handsome young man at the wheel of his own roadster. Someone usually brought a Kodak box camera, and friends posed at each other's homes and at scenic stop-offs to have their pictures made with the wonderful cars.

Finding several of those photographs in old albums has been enlightening and interesting. They were made in the late 1930s and through the summer of that fateful year of 1941. From the clothing worn by young ladies and gentlemen to the vintage automobiles, the history is fascinating.

35. This young man was very fashionably dressed during the Great Depression, especially in Appalachia. Double-breasted suits and two-tone, wingtip shoes were the latest styles. He is standing in front of a 1936 Ford Deluxe Touring Sedan. Notice a second vehicle in the background; it is a 1929 Chrysler.

The suave fellow in the double-breasted suit, white shirt, tie, and two-tone, wingtip shoes could well be some local person's great-grandfather. During the Great Depression, especially in Appalachia, he would have been extremely well-dressed, and quite sporty in such fashionable clothes. In fact, double-breasted suits were the latest trend. They had been newly revived during the 1920s and 1930s, having not been stylish since Prince Albert popularized the look in the mid-1800s.

The renewed design remained popular through the 1950s, and in difficult economic times of the 1930s, a double-breasted suit was high fashion. So were the two-tone, wing-tip shoes. Black-and-white or brown-and-white shoes had become popular when the Prince of Wales began wearing that style in the 1920s. And they were further promoted when Fred Astaire wore them while he danced in movies. Young folks in our mountains were staying current with the times.

In searching for clothing styles worn by the girls, I discovered an almost-identical coat in a vintage catalog. The teenaged girl standing by the 1931 Model-A Ford Deluxe Coupe was definitely wearing a fashionable winter coat, most likely ordered from Sears-Roebuck.

36. *These fashionably dressed children are posing beside a 1931 Model-A Ford Deluxe Coupe. The older girl's winter coat is similar to styles shown in Sears-Roebuck catalogs of that era. The little boy is wearing a double-breasted suit that was the latest trend at the time.*

However, socks worn with high-heeled shoes (shown in these photographs as well as in others throughout the book) would not necessarily have been by choice. Silk or rayon hosiery was expensive and impractical for mountain girls, and stockings were becoming increasingly unavailable at any price. Since the United States was preparing for a possible war, the government needed those raw materials.

Nevertheless, the button-front, summer dresses with belts are similar to styles shown in catalogs of the era. They appear to be classic 1930s fashions that remained popular for several years. Dresses in the early 1920s had been almost ankle-length, loosely fitted, and without defined waists. But times had changed, and longer hemlines quickly became outdated. Even in our secluded mountains, girls chose a more-modern look. Dresses and skirts were much prettier, shorter, and shapelier by the late 1930s.

It is easy to imagine that old-fashioned mothers might have been quite concerned about their daughters wearing "short" dresses and riding in fast roadsters driven by boys. In the old days, "courting" visits were in the front parlor under the watchful eye of the mother. A Sunday-afternoon drive was in a horse and buggy—without the dangers posed by new-fangled automobiles speeding around mountain-sides on narrow roads.

With their mothers' permission (hopefully) these young people were enjoying pleasant Sunday-afternoon drives. But that carefree era would be forever changed when Pearl Harbor was bombed. It is great to think they had these good times before the war and that the recovering economy enabled their friends to own and operate vehicles.

In preparing this article, it has been helpful to have the expert assistance of Roland and Lois Hoots, members of the Carolina Mountain Car Club. They are quite knowledgeable about antique cars, and I appreciate their information about the makes and models.

Think about Depression-era stories and pictures that have been passed down in your family. The late 1930s was a special time. Just before the harsh reality of World War

II, young people had the opportunity to wear the fashions of the day and to gather with friends. They felt privileged to enjoy scenic, Sunday-afternoon drives in Model-A Fords and other older cars.

Home gardens like Granny's are a renewed tradition in summer, 2020.

Since the mid-March Coronavirus quarantine, we have experienced empty shelves and purchasing limits at grocery stores. Millions of Americans staying home during the emerging springtime immediately thought of growing their own vegetables in the backyard. In fact, home gardens haven't been this popular since the Victory Garden campaign during World War II. Garden supply stores, near and far, have almost sold out of seeds, fertilizer, plants, trowels, and shovels.

Homegrown food was simply a way of life for Granny, and she couldn't have imagined not planting vegetables every year. Although she didn't talk specifically about Victory Gardens, I remember a day trip through lofty mountains near the Tennessee state line. As we admired the scenery, Granny was reminded of news programs she'd heard on the battery radio about overcrowded cities. She wondered aloud why thousands of people couldn't move to such isolated mountains and grow gardens. To her way of thinking, the idea seemed logical: they needed dependable access to food. And, as we crested yet another scenic mountaintop, she saw "plenty" of land.

37. From the 1880s to the 1980s, Granny lived in Henderson County and grew gardens most of her life. A calm, hard-working lady, she went about daily farm tasks determinedly and with a gentle spirit. Throughout two world wars, the 1918 flu pandemic, and the Great Depression, she found solace in planting and harvesting vegetables to feed her family. Gardeners in all eras have experienced peace, tranquility, and a sense of control over uncontrollable world situations as they till the soil.

Bear Mountain wasn't as tall as those we were admiring, but it was almost as inaccessible. There was no road to Granny's house, so we walked a mile-long trail through the forest from the nearest highway. She grew vegetables on a mountainside without a road, electricity, or modern conveniences, so she knew it was possible. Of course, she didn't understand national park lands or the concept of preserving wilderness environments. But country folks like Granny had always been extremely practical, and they probably could have solved many of the world's problems with their personal work ethic and wisdom.

For families with backyards, Granny certainly would have encouraged the idea of planting a garden. Stories of WWII Victory Gardens describe successful rooftop gardens for apartment buildings (which would have been inconceivable to her). But one way or another, 20 million determined Americans—many of whom were first-time gardeners—produced almost 40 percent of fresh vegetables used on the Homefront during that long war. Although nearly four billion jars and cans of food were preserved in 1943, a government-sponsored slogan urged people to "Grow more—Can more in '44."

Like Granny, those productive gardeners served summertime squash, okra, corn-on-the-cob, slicing tomatoes, and green beans; then they canned food for the coming winter.

Gardening was familiar in rural areas where much of the U.S. population still lived back then, but Victory Gardens confirmed that even townspeople could grow a lot of their own food.

A fascinating historical fact is that President Roosevelt's successful gardening campaign in 1942 was actually reminiscent of the earlier WWI "Sow the Seeds of Victory" promotion. Although it was not as well known or remembered, the 1917 initiative was also presented at schools. The Federal Bureau of Education promoted the U.S. School Garden Army (USSGA) in which children were enlisted as "Soldiers of the Soil." The energizing "soldier" designation motivated kids to help win the war, too.

Combined with the efforts of their parents and the general population, 3 million new garden plots were planted in 1917. And by the next year, there were 5.2 million home and community gardens. In addition to families enjoying fresh vegetables all summer, an estimated 1.45 million quarts of food were canned for winter. Presidents Wilson and Roosevelt knew that Americans growing a lot of their own food allowed more resources for our troops and allies during both world wars.

38. Myron Steppe has planted this garden in Flat Rock for over 20 years as an enjoyable hobby and in memory of his grandparents' fresh-sliced tomatoes and cucumbers. "That is a taste you never forget," he says. Although his parents considered a suitable garden to be at least 5 acres, Mr. Steppe continues the family tradition in a fenced-in portion of his backyard. This year he has Big Boy tomatoes (his mother's preference), summer and fall squash, cucumbers, assorted peppers, and sunflowers (his grandmother's favorite flower).

That long-ago tradition is being revived in the uncertain times of 2020. Granny would be pleased that here on Bear Mountain, spring onions are maturing, tomato plants are climbing faster than they can be tied up, and the beans are growing taller every day. It is interesting to contemplate what she would think of our modern, raised-bed gardens, but she'd certainly appreciate fresh vegetables.

The concept of home greenhouses is being successfully attempted for the first time by some of our area neighbors, as well. Granny would certainly have approved of such inno-vation, and I can only imagine her excitement at enjoying even-earlier springtime vegetables.

39. *The Albertson Homestead: In East Flat Rock, Josh and Annie are experimenting with a home greenhouse for the first time. They started vegetables from seed, and now have flourishing plants in an organic garden: broccoli, cauliflower, carrots, cabbage, tomatoes, watermelon, cantaloupe, cucumbers, pumpkins, jalapeños, onions, lavender, sage, peppermint, rosemary, leek, lettuce, beans, okra, Bok Choy, Swiss Chard, zucchini, and squash with pallet trellises. On less than a half-acre, they are creating a Back-to-Eden lifestyle that includes chickens, ducks, goats, and a pig.*

40. Three generations of family gardeners: In Zirconia, Mr. Donald Mullinax,
age 93, has planted this garden for 50 years, and it is growing again
this year with the help of his son, Terry, and Eagle Scout grandson,
Jonathan. Over time, he has shortened the rows and reduced the varieties,
but he always returns to the soil in springtime. This year they will
harvest beans, corn, okra, squash, onions, cucumbers, and tomatoes.
The picturesque garden has adequate sunshine, and he pumps irrigation
water from the creek. A picnic table underneath tall trees is perfect
for sampling a fresh cucumber after hoeing on a hot day.

Gardeners of all ages and in all eras have experienced a level of personal satisfaction and accomplishment that was evident in Granny's peaceful life. A calm, hard-working lady, she went about daily farm tasks determinedly and with a gentle spirit. The reliability and natural progression of the four seasons on Bear Mountain provided emotional stability and a sense of control over uncontrollable world situations.

*41. Wartime Victory Gardens were planted in both rural and city areas,
and in 2020 the tradition has been revived. In her deck garden,
Ellen McKinley Hughes grows tomatoes, green onions, green beans,
peppers, cucumbers, and a variety of herbs.*

After 1928, when they bought a new-fangled battery radio, Granny avidly listened to daily world-news broadcasts. Throughout the Great Depression, the shock of Pearl Harbor, and the long war, the news was increasingly disheartening, frightening, and often terrifying. Yet, as spring came again, Granny returned to the familiarity of planting vegetables to sustain her family. The predictable rhythm of the seasons calmed her spirit and soothed her soul even as overseas bombs dropped on allies and enemies alike.

Since "store-bought" groceries were rationed during wartime, she managed with reduced quantities of their beloved coffee and other favored treats. Like other committed Americans, Granny willingly did her part to sacrifice for the war effort. Special permits allowed for the purchase of extra sugar for home canning, and thankfully, she had a cow for milk and butter. Instead of depending on the limited accessibility of even more rationed items, farm folks raised hogs for meat and cooking fat.

We can only wonder how Granny would deal with the new, invisible enemy of Coronavirus. The closest comparison might be the 1918 worldwide influenza pandemic. Although nearly 200 cases were reported in the nearby community of Tuxedo, she somehow remained healthy. Perhaps the remoteness of Bear Mountain protected her, much like our recent quarantine on that same mountain. Even with modern roads these days, it offers some measure of safety and seclusion.

As the sun warmed the ground for another growing season, Granny always returned to the garden. Farm folks never strayed far from the land because they were nurtured by its bounty. Tilling the soil and enjoying the fruits of that labor is an agrarian concept much older than the towering office buildings and sprawling manufacturing facilities of modern times. Mountain people gained ageless wisdom and experience, and some of their practical insights remain valuable even in our high-tech world. In July, for example, it is good to know there is still time to plant a fall crop of turnip greens the way Granny did.

Self-reliance regarding food security hasn't been as valued as it once was, but empty grocery shelves remind us of its importance. For many, the response has been a renewed interest in home gardening and food preservation. In fact, so many freezers have been ordered that some stores have a six-month waiting list. While filling our new freezer, I am amused to realize that Granny would have considered it a catastrophe if her vegetables had frozen. Admittedly, most of us are not as pragmatic as our ancestors, but any efforts are beneficial. Gardens express individual personalities, and as these photos show, there is not "one correct way" to plant a garden. Since Victory Garden slogans were motivating, perhaps we can adopt a new one: "Grow Plenty in 2020."

Recall your grandparents' vegetable gardens, their work ethic, and long-ago examples of their resourcefulness during difficult times. It might be interesting to share those memories with younger generations, along with older relatives' stories about Victory Gardens and wartime food rationing.

We certainly have a long and enduring heritage of hardiness, adaptability, and strength.

Turtles enjoyed garden tomatoes, too

Planted on May 10, the traditional date to avoid frost in the mountains, fresh tomatoes were a mid-summer and early-fall treat in Granny's garden. Because they were the most important soup ingredient, she canned over 50 quarts each year. A good portion of the annual garden was set aside for favorite varieties of heirloom tomatoes, since Granny enjoyed having plenty for summertime slicing, too.

42. Turtles still like tomatoes on Bear Mountain.

143

Grandpa didn't like to find little, round holes chewed in his delicious, vine-ripened tomatoes, but this was a common occurrence on their mountain. Turtles, called "terrapins" by mountain folk, seemed to favor that lush habitat, and they especially liked the garden during tomato harvest.

When Grandpa brought in a bucket of fresh "maters" for Granny to can, he'd tell her, "There'd have been more, but the terrapins got there 'afore I did this mornin'."

Since he didn't want to harm the turtles, Grandpa carried them down below the barn away from the garden. But, by the next morning, they were back again—munching on his tasty tomatoes. Frustrated, he started carrying them farther and farther away. He couldn't tell if this was doing any good, though, since he didn't know which ones found their way back.

Finally, he came up with an idea that turned the problem into a fun hobby that he really enjoyed during his retirement years. Grandpa painted a different red X or other identification mark on each turtle's shell. Then, he carried them a mile or more into the forest before setting them down.

When he returned to the house, he noted the information on the calendar. Afterward, he counted the days until the same turtles reappeared in his garden. That way he could follow their movements.

Some actually made the long journey in about three weeks. Grandpa got a lot of enjoyment out of looking for the different turtles as he gathered fresh tomatoes. He enjoyed the turtle-free days too, while they were making their way back to the garden. Apparently, they remembered dining on his juicy tomatoes.

Since early settlers thought tomatoes were decorative but too poisonous for human consumption, turtles may have developed a never-to-be-forgotten taste for the delightful summertime treat.

In later years, wildlife experts have used miniature radio transmitters to track turtles on the mountain. Their movements can be followed by computers from miles away. In an era when some species could eventually become extinct, such scientific information is useful for long-term studies.

Grandpa's reason for tracking the turtles, however, was more immediate. He wanted to make sure his sun-ripened tomatoes didn't become "extinct"—before he had a chance to eat them.

Traditionally, vegetables grown at home were essential to mountain folks' year-round food supply, so protecting the harvest was an ongoing task. Think of stories about your ancestors who dealt with unwelcome animals in their vegetable gardens.

Daytime programs on the battery radio filled long afternoons with drama

43. *Country Hawkins "listens" to his antique radio from the 1920s.
Grandpa's first radio may have been similar to this one.
Notice the separate speaker on the radio cabinet.*

Grandpa bought the "new-fangled" battery radio in 1928 primarily to hear the *Grand Ole Opry*. Over the years he and Granny came to enjoy the daytime programming, as well. She always had favorite soap operas that ended with the tantalizing words, "Tune in again tomorrow for the next exciting episode…." After Grandpa's retirement from the railroad, the radio provided afternoon entertainment for him, as well.

Unchanged from his working years, their mornings still began at 4 a.m. Granny and Grandpa liked to complete farm chores, hoe the garden, carry water, and chop wood before the sun became too hot. By midafternoon, they had worked more hours than a modern person's full-time job. So, they were ready to rest in their favorite living room chairs and listen to the radio. During my week-long, summer visits to the Bear Mountain farm, I looked forward to those afternoon programs, too.

My grandparents' favorite show was *Art Linkletter's House Party,* especially the ongoing contest, "Guess What's in the House." Mr. Linkletter gave hints and studio audience members volunteered guesses. Each wrong answer made the prize more valuable, and he reiterated the instructions: The household item inside the small, model house was of actual size; it would be commonly used and instantly recognizable.

Grandpa enjoyed guessing, and one time he was right. The contest, however, didn't have a winner, and the prize climbed to hundreds of dollars. Nobody could guess the common item inside the little house, except Grandpa.

Of course, his answer didn't count on a prerecorded radio broadcast from California, but he had a lot of fun, anyway. He laughed and declared, "When somebody finally guesses what's in the house, it will be a Thermos bottle."

The contest lasted several weeks before one lucky person realized the mystery item was, indeed, a Thermos bottle.

I remember Grandpa's smug grin when the winner was announced. And he enjoyed telling that story for several years.

The comical answers on the "Kids Say the Darndest Things" segment were always entertaining. Grandpa especially liked Art Linkletter's question, "What did your parents tell you not to say?" The live audience roared with merriment, and we did, too.

Granny enjoyed Fashion Designer Edith Head's guidance when ladies in Mr. Linkletter's audience asked her expert opinion. Miss Head offered advice to help ordinary women look slimmer, younger, and more fashionable.

Granny leaned forward and listened eagerly as she visualized the live, studio scene. Short, older ladies like her were advised not to wear horizontal stripes, gathered skirts, loud colors, or hats with tall feathers. Granny felt more confident about her own clothing style when she realized she already followed those fashion rules.

The soap operas Granny enjoyed also became Grandpa's favorites. *Hilltop House* with narratives about Miss Julie taking care of the orphans filled long, weekday afternoons with warmth, drama, and apprehension.

Granny became quite concerned when Miss Julie received an unexpected job offer. Almost immediately, several "mean ole ladies" began applying to be the new manager of Hilltop House. I remember Granny lamenting about "them pore little young'uns." One applicant after another was totally unsuited for the position (in Granny's opinion).

Still, for a long time, it sounded like Miss Julie might leave the orphanage. Every day when the problem was unresolved, the program ended with, "Tune in again tomorrow for the next exciting episode...."

After what seemed like forever, Miss Julie realized she couldn't abandon the children to the care of an unqualified administrator. Granny was vastly relieved that none of the candidates had seemed trustworthy to Miss Julie, either.

Granny knew Miss Julie wasn't a real person like Art Linkletter, but she enjoyed a good story that demonstrated integrity. Speaking in distinctive Appalachian English, Granny told me, "Miss Julie shore done the right thing." Looking back, I realize Granny was teaching life lessons, and it is remarkable that she used examples from an old-time, radio drama.

Bear Mountain was so secluded that electricity would not become available until 1975, decades after Grandpa's life-time. So, in the mid-1950s, when most local folks watched television, Grandpa and Granny still relied on the battery radio. It brought daily entertainment, laughter, fashion, and drama from faraway places to their living room. They never got over their excitement and always looked forward to the next installments of favorite shows.

Grandpa bought many of the products that sponsored those programs, too. Considering the numerous clean-ing items that were advertised, soap operas were correctly named: Rinso and Oxydol detergents, Old Dutch Cleanser, and Lifebuoy, Palmolive, and Ivory bath soaps. Granny and Grandpa never could decide if Palmolive soap was better than 99 $^{44}/_{100}$% Pure Ivory, so they used both brands.

They enjoyed Carnation evaporated milk, Martha White Self-Rising Flour with Hot Rize, Quaker Oats, Nabisco crackers, Hadacol, Carter's Little Liver Pills, Vaseline, and other highly promoted items.

Radio advertising was quite effective in those days. Grandpa would ask for specific brands at Maybin's Grocery in Zirconia, and he always wanted Maxwell House Coffee. If coffee prices spiked, he would substitute instant Postum, but he always went back to his favorite coffee.

In the "Golden Age of Radio" other popular programs included *Fibber McGee and Molly, The Abbott and Costello Show, The Lone Ranger, The Roy Rogers Show, Lum and Abner,* and *Amos and Andy.* Several mysteries were broadcast, including *The New Adventures of Sherlock Holmes* and *The Shadow.*

However, Granny didn't care much for scary programs like *The Shadow.* The narrator's evil laugh and menacing tone would have kept her up at night. Sinister plots of murder, mayhem, and bloodshed were not Granny's idea of entertainment. It is interesting that she lived on an isolated mountain—inhabited by poisonous snakes and wild animals—without any fear. But frightful laughter, screams, and gunshots coming from inside the wooden radio cabinet would have terrified her.

Realistic sound effects, often accompanied by eerie organ music, made such programs spellbinding in the days when radio was new. In fact, engineers were still learning to imitate thuds, crashes, thunder, horses, and other noises required for various scripts. They experimented with common objects since radio audiences couldn't see what was happening in the studio.

One of the earliest successes was the rhythm of galloping horses created by clapping coconut shells on a board. Squeezing a box of cornstarch suggested footsteps in snow, and scrunching cellophane near a microphone represented a crackling fire. For the more ominous sound of a person being stabbed, a knife was forcefully plunged into a cabbage (accompanied by a soundman's bloodcurdling scream).

No wonder Granny was particular about which programs she listened to, but she always enjoyed the soft, melodious organ music that introduced her soap operas.

Their nearest neighbor lived a mile through the forest, but on lonely, weekday afternoons my grandparents were connected to the outside world. Through the wonder of a battery-operated radio, they heard laughter and applause all the way from California. And on occasion, I was fortunate to be there and experience the drama with them.

In the "Golden Age of Radio," your grandparents probably enjoyed programs that ended with, "Tune in again tomorrow for the next exciting episode…." Try to recall family stories about their favorite shows and their comments about early dramas or comedies.

Ask some of the oldest people you know if they remember highly advertised products like Rinso detergent, Hadacol, or Postum.

Small Coronavirus weddings recall Granny's memories of old-time ceremonies

During Coronavirus, the $74 billion wedding industry is adjusting to a 90 percent reduction with postponements, cancellations, or at best, extreme downsizing. Instead of the previous $34,000 average cost, some brides are creatively opting for "minimonies" with just a few guests in the backyard. Although such drastic changes are unsettling and disappointing, this trend recalls Granny's memories of simple weddings she attended in the late 1800s.

As a little girl, I remember listening with eager attentiveness to her quaint stories about old-fashioned brides. From childhood, Granny's home church was Crossroads Baptist in rural Zirconia. After the sermon, the minister would make the usual altar call for those in the small congregation who wanted prayer. Then, he would ask if anyone wished to join the church.

But one Sunday in 1896, Granny recalled, the pastor additionally inquired, "Is there a couple who would like to be married? If so, please come forward at this time."

To Granny's surprise, a young man and his girlfriend stepped into the aisle, walked to the altar, and stood facing the minister. He calmly asked them to join hands as he intoned the traditional vows: "Do you take this woman to be thy lawfully wedded wife, to have and to hold from this day forward…till death do us part, according to God's holy law…."

But not every couple back then followed the man-made law (enacted in 1870) to register marriages in North Carolina. As Granny reminisced, she enjoyed speculating about a marriage license for a spur-of-the-moment wedding. She mulled over the possibility that the pastor was also surprised, "Do you suppose he knowed about the weddin' ahead of time?" Then, Granny merrily wondered aloud, "Reckon he'd ever made that kind of altar call before?"

Her engaging story-telling skills added intrigue to the unusual wedding, and I tried to imagine the astonishment of the congregation. Like Granny, they weren't expecting a marriage ceremony after the worship service. What an exciting day in that mountain church—a wedding during an altar call became the "talk of the country."

The 21st century "surprise wedding" is not new, after all. It is interesting to hear about close friends arriving at an engagement party—and attending the wedding instead. To expedite a forthcoming marriage (especially during Coronavirus), surprise weddings have become one possible option. And Granny attended a surprise wedding in the 1890s.

She also talked about a country-farm wedding in that same era. Following a front-porch ceremony, the bride's mother served an outdoor dinner for kinfolks and neighbors. Then, Granny remembered seeing the couple leave in a pioneer-style, covered wagon. Pulled by strong mules, it was loaded with household furnishings and provisions of food for the long trip to Georgia where they would live. As a child, Granny had no idea how far they were going. In native Appalachian English, she told me, "I knowed it musta been a long ways 'cause it took'em 20 years to come back to North Carolina, and they's still ridin' in a wagon."

When automobiles became popular, Granny sometimes traveled to Georgia. But she always maintained the idea that it was a long way from home. On a much later occasion when I was organist for a church service in North Georgia, Granny thought I should have left hours earlier. She kept saying, "Won't you be late? It's a long ways to Georgia." When I assured her I was on schedule, she jokingly retold the wagon story.

Decades after modern roads and transportation, she enjoyed reminiscing about the bride and groom who returned from Georgia 20 years later—still riding in a wagon. Granny's stories were always entertaining, and her memories were uniquely descriptive of Appalachian weddings in the 1800s.

The almost-clandestine plan for Granny's own wedding was equally fascinating. By 1909, local couples had learned to avoid the "red tape" required by North Carolina's 1870 marriage-license law. Mountain people have always disliked bureaucracy; they preferred keeping important dates in the family Bible.

South Carolina didn't require marriage licenses until 1911, so the North and South Carolina state line became a popular wedding venue in the early 1900s. Quite conveniently, Henderson County borders South Carolina. So, on their appointed wedding day, Granny and Grandpa walked four miles to meet the minister at the state line.

44. This 1908 photograph shows Granny and Grandpa (standing on the back row) before they were married. It is likely that they wore these Sunday clothes to their 1909 wedding at the North Carolina and South Carolina state line.

Even then, the boundary between the two states was clearly marked. As the outdoor ceremony began, the bride, groom, minister, and a couple of witnesses carefully stepped into South Carolina. (One can imagine that a miniature park was eventually flattened by footprints from weddings performed there.) Since no marriage laws were in place, the minister declared Granny and Grandpa to be husband and wife at the conclusion of their vows. And, without being licensed by either of the two states, my grandparents' marriage lasted forty-seven years until Grandpa's death in 1956.

45. *Posing beside a 1935 Plymouth, this is possibly a wedding photo of Janie Mae's parents in 1942. She seldom wore hats, but she is wearing a white dress with a matching white hat, and he is in his Army uniform. They were married at the Greenville (South Carolina) County Court House during a short Army furlough.*

For many more decades, South Carolina maintained fewer wedding restrictions than North Carolina. When my parents married in 1942, they drove to the Greenville County Court House during a brief Army furlough before his South Pacific deployment. Like other Henderson County couples, they were granted a same-day wedding without a waiting period or the medical examination required in their own state.

Granny was understandably distraught, and years later told me, "I wasn't expectin' them to get married, so I believed their made-up story about goin' to a Jones family reunion." It took Granny a long time to come to terms with their wedding, and she wasn't alone. Nationwide records for 1942 indicate an 83 percent increase in marriages from pre-war years, and many such couples also eloped before overseas' assignments. To parental dismay, young ladies quickly followed the wartime fad of having a husband in the service. APO/FPO love letters and souvenirs from faraway places were highly prized and became instant status symbols.

The Greenville County Court House was also an expedient, inexpensive wedding venue during those difficult years of the Great Depression. There are stories in Henderson County of successful marriages (lasting over 60 years) that began with flagging down the morning Greyhound on U.S. Hwy. 25. For young folks without cars, the southbound bus was a quick, reliable way to elope; they could be married by mid-day and return on the afternoon Greyhound. Those who owned vehicles would drive to Greenville but determined young couples didn't let lack of transportation stop their plans.

Sometimes families knew of a daughter's engagement, but more often they did not. There were amusing stories of underage brides telling the judge they were "between 18 and 19." What the girl actually meant was the number 18 was written on a slip of paper inside her hat. The number 19 was printed on another piece of paper tucked in her shoe. So, the would-be bride was "between 18 and 19." (However, it is doubtful that an experienced judge would believe such a fib.)

Like the harsh realities of Appalachian farm life, the Great Depression, and Pearl Harbor, Coronavirus may have changed the concept of huge, elaborate weddings for some time to come. Mirroring those eras of war and economic uncertainty, "microweddings" and "minimonies" could become the new-normal.

Think about long-ago elopements, simple ceremonies, non-traditional venues, wartime, or surprise weddings in your family history. Recalling the courage and ingenuity of our ancestors is certainly a positive approach in these difficult times. "Creatively modified" weddings featuring lovely brides continue to be celebrated in 2020. We can be thankful for the joy these determined couples find in their new lives together—even during a worldwide pandemic.

Fourth of July
in the Country

46. Janie Mae's brother, James Evance Jones, age 3,
eating watermelon at the Lemmon's Hole on the Fourth of July.

L ocal folks in the late 1940s and early 1950s were quite
fearful of Fourth of July traffic. They'd already seen the
mangled, twisted cars piled near busy intersections. In those
days, the county sheriff purposely displayed automobiles
from really bad wrecks to forewarn holiday speeders. Certain
that death and destruction lurked around every curve, some

mountain people just refused to drive on the highway from July 3rd to 5th.

Fortunately, there was a dirt lane behind U.S. Staton's country store near Tuxedo. Uneasy customers drove on secondary roads, parked in the ditch, and walked down the hill to shop for necessities. They completely avoided busy U.S. Highway 25 – until it was safe again.

For holiday entertainment, it was quite exciting to buy an ice-cold watermelon and carry it to the truck. Then, the whole family enjoyed a trip (on gravel roads) to the Lemmon's Hole. A Kodak box camera preserved the day on black-and-white film as the "young'uns" ate watermelon slices on the sandy shores of Green River.

The Lemmon's Hole was a long, partly shaded bend in the river that temporarily slowed the current on its way toward Saluda. Summer limbs, heavy with tangled green vines, drooped near the surface and reflected dimly in the calm water. A story from the 1800s recalled Mr. Lemmon driving a wagon and a team of horses on a stormy night. As he attempted to cross the flooded river, the wagon washed downstream. Afterward, that section of Green River became known as the Lemmon's Hole. Country churches conducted outdoor baptism services there, since in later years it was not deep enough to be popular for swimming.

However, the Lemmon's Hole was so highly favored for trout fishing that locals crowded both banks. Everybody wanted to hook the elusive Rainbow Trout, but they were quite happy to take home a string of tasty Brown Trout. On July Fourth, only a few minnows darted in sunlit ripples close to shore, so it was the strange name and sinister history that fascinated mountain children. They imagined what might have happened to Mr. Lemmon. Maybe he actually survived, after all.

In an era of theme-park vacations, how many folks recall the simplicity of sitting beside a lazy river on July Fourth, eating watermelon with old-fashioned Mamas and Daddies—who were too scared to drive on a two-lane highway?

During August, Granny was busy canning garden vegetables

Augustus was perhaps the busiest month of the year for Granny. The harvest seemed to ripen all at once, and she needed to "put it away for the winter." That was an expression used to describe pickling and canning in the days when mountain folks lived off the land. She preserved fruits and vegetables in hundreds of "fruit jars" and stored them on the can-house shelves.

Granny often told me the story of learning, as a young bride, to use sunny days in March to cut a summer's supply of stove wood. Being inexperienced at managing a farm while Grandpa was working on the railroad, she often ran short of wood. It was easy to underestimate the amount required to keep the cook stove hot all day during canning season, so she learned by trial and error in those early years.

In fact, the whole idea of home canning was in the early stages back then. Like learning to keep enough wood on hand, the skills of preserving foods in glass jars were acquired by experimenting. It is amazing how well the young, mountain women learned rather-complicated, new techniques.

As a child, I remember asking Great-Grandma Alice Pace (1874-1968) how farm ladies in her era learned to can fruits and vegetables. She was a generation older than Granny, and I was fascinated with her knowledge about old-time skills.

47. Great-Grandma Alice A. Pace (1874-1968)

As Great-Grandma tipped back and forth in her rocking chair on the country porch, she remembered, "Well, it was a lot like modern (1950s) women are learning to use home freezers. Back then, we tried one way, and if it didn't work, we tried a different way. Then we talked about our experiences with our neighbors and learned from one another.

"Back in the late 1800s," Great-Grandma Pace explained, "my friends would tell me they processed some vegetables a lot longer than others to make the jars seal. So, the next summer, I'd try it that way, too. Eventually we learned to can better in the summer, so we had plenty to eat all winter."

Her story was fascinating, and the long history of home canning certainly bears out her concept of experimentation. In fact, the idea goes back to 1795 when Napoleon Bonaparte offered a reward to anyone who could develop a way to preserve food for his army.

A local French chef, Nicholas Appert, took on the challenge. Being experienced in making candy, wine, and pickles, he knew more about food preservation than most people. Still, he practiced over a decade to develop a method for canning food in airtight, glass jars. Chef Appert collected the prize, but he wouldn't live long enough to understand why his idea of boiling the filled jars worked. A fellow Frenchman, Louis Pasteur, solved the mystery of microorganisms and bacteria when he discovered food pasteurization in the early 1860s.

Across the ocean, John L. Mason of New York City, invented the Mason canning jar in the late 1850s. His jar had the first screw-on thread moulded into the rim, and it featured a reusable, metal lid secured with a rubber seal. Mr. Mason, however, eventually sold his rights to the Mason jar and died a poor man.

In 1869, Lewis R. Boyd patented a glass-lined lid that prevented food from coming in contact with metal, and the concept was used for decades. In the early 1880s, a newer invention, the so-called "lightning jar," became popular. It was named for the reusable glass lid and attached wire clamp that sealed quickly—like lightning. "Strong Shoulder" Atlas jars were developed because their stronger rims resisted cracking (a common problem of earlier glass jars).

Home canning had become widely accepted after the Civil War, partly because of the growing popularity and convenience of wood cook stoves. Ladies could now cook at waist height versus bending over the fireplace, plus the stove provided a level surface for heavy pots filled with jars. Improved and marketed during that era, these two helpful, consumer items came together to benefit average housewives. This post-war interaction of canning jars and cook stoves offers an opportunity to recall their combined contributions to our ancestors' lifestyles.

By 1886, the successful Ball brothers began buying smaller, glass-jar companies. Alexander Kerr offered the first wide-mouth jars in 1903, and he later invented the two-part lid that is still used today.

It is thought-provoking to realize that wood stoves were once highly desired kitchen appliances. And during Great-Grandma Pace's early adulthood, canning jars and lids were still being perfected. Those innovations remained the most advanced—and complicated—methods of food preservation during Granny's generation, as well.

Mountain ladies learned by trial and error to keep the fires burning, and to sterilize jars, rubber-sealing bands, and lids. The length of time required to boil jars of vegetables and fruits to seal them was crucial. Home-canned corn was one of the most dangerous foods to preserve safely. Yet I remember dozens of quarts of corn on Granny's can-house shelves. Another difficult and risky farm product was fresh sausage made at hog-killing time. Granny successfully pre-served many jars of sausage (though as a small child, I didn't think her canned sausage looked very tasty).

Fruits, berries, and tomatoes were packed in jars and pro-cessed in pots of steaming water for the shortest times; beans and beets required longer boiling. The popping sounds of cooling jars were music to the ears of ladies who had spent hours over a hot stove.

Modern people might barely recognize "Mason" jar names like Atlas, Ball, and Kerr, but those brands were com-mon during my childhood. I recall Granny using several types of lids, including glass tops secured with wire clamps. She favored old-style, metal lids with milk-glass liners, and

I have a few of them that were eventually discarded around the home place. Granny disliked the two-piece, metal tops and bands that are still used today. She didn't think they sealed as well as her traditional, glass-lined lids.

As Great-Grandma Pace mentioned, home freezing was just becoming popular in the 1950s, though it wasn't an option on Bear Mountain. Even if electricity had been available, I imagine that Granny would have lost sleep worrying about a power outage.

Like other old-time, farm ladies, she knew her summer's work was well preserved in "fruit jars" in the can house. Built almost underground, it protected glass jars, as well as potatoes, pumpkins, apples, and onions from freezing during winter. In fact, if any of Granny's food had frozen, it would have been a catastrophe.

Mountain ladies would preserve as much of the harvest as possible, including the last beans on the vines and apples that had fallen to the ground. While trimming rotten spots, they'd sometimes joke, "Well, this ain't the best, but it'll taste better than a snowball next winter."

Granny's can house has been left to time, the wind, and the seasons. The sturdy, wooden structure that Grandpa built so long ago has fallen and rotted away. But the three-sided indention—that he dug by hand into the hillside—is still visible. And it is recognizable to those who remember the old ways.

You may have stories about your grandparents' well-stocked, can houses that you could share with younger generations. Do any of your August memories involve woodstoves, gardens, "putting foods away for the winter," or home canning? Think of brands of "Mason" jars that you recall, along with different types of jar lids that you remember.

Pure Sourwood honey continues to be a unique, mountain favorite

Mountain beekeepers jokingly declared, "Five times as much Sourwood honey has been sold as was ever made by the bees." That's because they knew their own honey was pure Sourwood. It's long been a matter of personal pride in the mountains to gather both wildflower and Sourwood honey. Both flavors are tasty and healthful, of course, but it is important for older mountainfolk to distinguish between the two.

Enjoying Sourwood, as well as wildflower honey, is one of the advantages of living in Appalachia. The Sourwood tree (*Oxydendrum arboretum*) is native to the Eastern United States. Western North Carolinians are proud that "honey trees" are most prolific in our area and in North Georgia. Over the years, Sourwood has become known as "the honey with a Southern accent," and most people would agree.

In fact, Sourwood trees are so special, they are not native to any other part of the world. If trees are transplanted, however, they can live in areas where the climate and conditions are similar to their natural habitat in Appalachia.

The name, Sourwood comes from the acrid, bitter, and sour taste of the wood and leaves. Mountain climbers have chewed Sourwood leaves like chewing gum, or made leaf tea, to quench thirst on long hikes. Native Americans and pioneers used the tea for herbal remedies and nerve tonics that helped respiratory and stomach problems.

Aside from folkloric benefits, Sourwood is one of the most colorful trees in the fall. Those bitter leaves turn beautifully red, yellow, orange, and rust colors much earlier than others in the forest. Such bright foliage is delightful for seasonal decorations.

As trees go, the Sourwood is relatively small (usually not much taller than 50 to 60 feet with a 12- to 20-inch diameter trunk) but it makes up for size with the fragrance of its mid-summer flowers. Bees are drawn to seven-inch stems of creamy-white, hanging blooms that individually look like tiny bells. Because of the resemblance of those little bells to the shape of garden lilies, the tree has also been called the Lily of the Valley tree and the Appalachian Lily tree.

Granny and Grandpa weren't familiar with those names, but they watched for Sourwood trees to blossom after many of the other flowers on remote Bear Mountain. Theirs was a perfect location because isolated beehives in the mountains are more likely to yield nectar almost exclusively from late-blooming Sourwood. Like other countryfolk, my grandparents prepared hives to receive the annual bounty by harvesting early honey before the Sourwoods bloomed. Replacing wooden frames inside the hives with fresh inserts would collect pure Sourwood honey.

48. *David Stallings checks a frame of Sourwood honey at Camp Falling Creek in Zirconia. For purer Sourwood honey, he transports beehives to 13 remote locations in Henderson and Transylvania Counties.*

49. *Sourwood honey from Mr. Stallings' Bee Masters Farm is available at Johnson Family Farm Produce, 1202 Kanuga Road.*

The resulting monofloral honey (versus polyfloral honey) is lighter in color, and the almost-clear tint characterizes Sourwood honey. Farm folks like my grandparents enjoyed it seasonally in addition to the tasty wildflower honey they'd already harvested.

Along with our traditional appreciation of fresh honey, the bees themselves are important to the natural ecosystem. So many fruits and vegetables could disappear without pollination that beekeepers actually transport hives to farms and orchards during springtime. The low survival rate of bees has been a worldwide concern, so experts like Steve Pettis of Henderson County Cooperative Extension office are glad for a slight improvement in 2020.

Commercially processed honey from other areas (perhaps other countries) just can't compare with the concentration of unfiltered, natural antioxidants in locally harvested wildflower or Sourwood honey. Connoisseurs like Mr. Pettis consider both flavors healthful because nature's local ingredients are better to alleviate symptoms of local allergies. That's why some folks take mountain honey by the spoonful at morning and night. While I am sure they must be right, my favorite way to eat honey is slathered on hot, buttered biscuits. Other tasty ideas include spooning it onto warm oatmeal or poking holes in a hot Bundt cake and drizzling honey overtop. By experimenting, cooks have learned to substitute honey for refined sugar to improve the taste, texture, and health benefits of favorite recipes.

50. *Jim Poe of Poe's Backyard Bees harvests honey from one of his 50 hives—in his backyard. Living in an urban area without nearby Sourwood trees, Mr. Poe specializes in fresh, mixed-wildflower honey. Becoming involved in local honey production several years ago after attending a Cooperative Extension Agency beekeeping class, he mentors others who are interested in learning.*

51. *Honey from Poe's Backyard Bees is shown with cantaloupe blooms. Notice the bee on the bloom in the inset. Pollination is necessary for fruits and vegetables, and bees play an important role in the natural ecosystem. Poe's Honey is available at Henderson County Cooperative Extension Office, 100 Jackson Park Road.*

And honey is one of the few, fresh foods that doesn't spoil for a long time (some folks say never). It may harden but returns to its liquid state after being warmed. As a naturally produced (versus man-made) food, honey has advocates among modern people as well as old-timers like Granny and Grandpa.

As a child I had to stay in the house while Granny "robbed" the beehives. Grandpa was working on the railroad, so it fell to Granny to harvest vegetables from the garden and to harvest honey from the hives, as well. The mountain term was "robbing the bee gums," and I guess the bees felt like they were being robbed.

Back then, country ladies wore cotton dresses, aprons, and old-fashioned bonnets when they worked in the garden. But before Granny took honey out of the hives, she put on two pairs of Grandpa's bib overalls, his oldest hat, a thick coat, gloves, and a special, hooded mask with a screened front.

Since she was a short lady and Grandpa was a tall man, I thought the overalls folded around her shoe tops in a most protective and amusing way. Her many-layered outfit looked quite comical and strange. But I understood why she wore so many clothes; at five years old, I'd already been bee stung a few times. And I could only imagine how mad the bees would be when Granny started taking the roofs off their houses and stealing their honey.

As I continued to watch in fascination and amazement, she stuffed old rags into the bee smoker and lit them with a match. Granny practiced squeezing the handle a few times to be sure it emitted enough smoke to confuse the bees. When she was satisfied it was working, she instructed me (in native Appalachian English), "Now, you be shore and stay in the house 'til I git back."

I always tried to do what Granny said, anyway, and was especially glad to obey her that time. I knew the bees would buzz and get real mad when they were disturbed. I'd seen hundreds of them flying in wild circles through the yard, and I certainly didn't want to be in their path.

But I could watch some of the exciting activity through the kitchen windows. It wasn't too long before Granny climbed the hill carrying a dishpan of fresh honey. She spent the afternoon ladling it, honeycomb and all, into wide-mouth canning jars. She and Grandpa were especially fond of crunchy honeycomb, as well as strained honey, on breakfast biscuits.

When the jars were full, she carried a few at a time to the can house. Thankfully, the bees had finally settled back down. I didn't see them zooming around as I tentatively followed her through the yard.

Granny set the Sourwood honey beside jars of fresh wildflower honey already on the shelves. My grandparents never had enough honey to sell, but there was plenty for their own use. Typically the supply lasted until time to "rob the bee gums" the next year.

The exciting day of angry bees and honey stealing had been memorable and entertaining for me; I had especially enjoyed the absurdity of seeing Granny dressed in Grandpa's clothes. And I already looked forward to breakfast biscuits—dripping with butter and honey.

You may have memories of Sourwood blooms and stories of "robbing" beehives, as well. Try to recall the details and share them with someone. Better still, bake some hot biscuits to serve with pure, mountain honey.

Dealing with weeds before chemicals.

B efore a few squirts of liquid weed killer would take care of summer weeds, my grandparents used a sling blade around the yard and the edges of the garden. That seemed to work well enough for their purposes, though the garden and corn fields had to be hoed quite often to keep weeds out and make a good crop.

Granny carefully hand-pulled every weed that dared to grow in her beloved flower garden. Her favorite way of showing disgust with the offensive plant was to vigorously shake the dirt off its roots and toss it to wither in the hot sun. That weed would never grow again, and she was glad!

Bigger than their personal struggles with weeds, however, were Grandpa's track duties with Southern Railway. Thick weeds and grass grew beside the railroad tracks, between the crossties, as well as around the rails and switches. Employees had to take time from their regular work to deal with this hazardous, ongoing problem at least twice during the growing season, and sometimes more often.

The train could actually slip and slide quite dangerously if long, slick grass accumulated between the wheels and the rail. Railroad men coined the term "grassing track" to describe these extra duties.

In the decades before chemical weed killer, the job was done by hand with grubbing hoes—mile after mile throughout the mountains, and across the United States. "Grassing track" was so arduous that a crew of six men using the available hand tools could clean less than one mile of railroad track in a day.

52. An unused, modern-day railroad shows how weeds can take over without modern chemicals or old-time trackmen to forcefully dig them.

This particular job seemed to be harder than replacing crossties, according to Grandpa's expressed level of exhaustion at the end of a day. Keeping Southern's busy railroads safe required thousands of manhours of hand grubbing throughout every growing season.

The first chemical weed killer became available as Grandpa was nearing retirement in the 1940s, so his working years always included the seasonal struggle with weeds and grass.

Homeowners and gardeners now have the option of using a commercial weed killer, and railroads benefit from modern developments, as well. As it was in Grandpa's era, vegetation management continues to be an important and essential component to railway maintenance and safety.

It is interesting to wonder what old-time trackmen would think about huge sprayer trucks fitted with railroad-wheel attachments. Modern-day drivers and operators ride down the tracks like a train, and easily spray weed killer, front, back, left and right.

Those hard workers from the past would probably stand and cheer!

Even without men with grubbing hoes laboriously "grassing track," there are still a lot of necessary jobs. Despite advancements and innovative equipment, the problem of weeds growing on the railroad must be dealt with at least twice a year, and sometimes more often—just like in the old days.

Some things never change.

The weeds keep coming back.

Finding a balance between the old methods and the new is particularly important when it comes to introducing more chemicals into our everyday lives.

Sometimes we need to spray, but it is still rewarding to pull weeds by hand, vigorously shake the dirt off their miserable roots—and toss them to wither in the hot sun!

Think about your worst (and best) experiences that involved weeds.

Chicken and dumplings
for Sunday dinner

Living on a secluded mountain, Granny welcomed company and began meal preparations well in advance. Sunday dinner, served in the middle of the day, certainly required an early start.

She gathered seasonal vegetables from the garden, picked fresh fruit for the cobbler, carried buckets of water from the spring and armloads of wood from the woodshed.

After decades of use, her 1910 wood-burning cook stove was still shiny black. With contrasting white-enamel doors, an oven temperature gauge, and a handy hot-water reservoir, it had been a top-of-the-line model in its day.

In her opinion, it still was.

Grandpa said food had to be cooked on a woodstove to be "fit to eat," and Granny agreed.

Along with bowls of summertime green beans, cornmeal-crusted okra, corn-on-the-cob, quick-fried cabbage, and vine-ripened, sliced tomatoes, her signature company dish was chicken and dumplings.

Unlike most of us, when Granny made this specialty, the first thing she did was go out in the yard and flag down a chicken. As a small child, I thought that part was fun. It was suddenly permissible to chase the chickens!

53. When I moved to Bear Mountain as an adult, I chose this chicken-design wall border for the kitchen in memory of Granny's Rhode Island Red chickens. I have been amused wondering what Granny would think. She'd say, "Pictures of chickens are purty, but where are your real chickens?" If I told her I didn't have any, she'd ask, "What do you cook for Sunday dinner? Where do you get eggs?" Granny would have a hard time understanding dependence on modern grocery stores—and during the 2020 Coronavirus pandemic when grocers' shelves have sometimes been empty, we can better understand her old-fashioned reasoning and concern.

It was always a comical sight, seeing my aged Granny running around the yard in her old-fashioned clunky, high-heeled shoes. She'd wildly wave her apron toward the one she'd selected for the place of honor on her Sunday table.

Since the chicken wasn't happy about her choice, it'd flap and squawk as we chased it from one end of the yard to the other.

Under the English boxwoods, through the edge of the flower bed, 'round and 'round the walnut tree we went—feathers flying, and all the other chickens raising the alarm and cackling, too, by now.

What a commotion on the normally peaceful mountain!

Finally cornering the chicken at the edge of the woodshed, Granny would wring its neck with a swift flick of her wrist. Sometimes she'd lay the chicken on the chopping block and whack its head off with the ax.

It'd flop and flail over the yard for a while, and then she'd dip the dead chicken in boiling water to make the job of plucking the feathers easier. Those she couldn't pluck, she singed off over open flames in the woodstove.

The next tasks were to clean the chicken and cut off the feet. Then, she was ready to begin simmering it in a big pot, and rolling out the tasty dumplings—all in time for the guests to arrive shortly after noon.

Describing this once-common farm process, so necessary to serve a chicken dinner, makes me wonder:

How many of us would be up to the task today?

A few older neighbors and kinfolk remember walking a mile through the woods to Grandpa and Granny's secluded mountain home place. They still talk about the delicious, chicken-and-dumpling Sunday dinners.

Like me, they haven't forgotten the fresh blackberry cobblers, crusty cornbread and fluffy biscuits—baked to perfection in the big, black woodstove.

Think of ancestral stories you may have heard about delicious meals prepared on similar old-fashioned stoves.

Recall and share memories of older relatives' signature company dishes—even if they didn't need to chase down a chicken first.

A wandering musician visits Bear Mountain

After an early Saturday supper, Grandpa liked to rest in his rocking chair and listen to the 6 o'clock news on the battery radio. It wasn't quite time for his favorite program, the *Grand Ole Opry*. So, when the news was over, he just took it easy after a long, hot day on the farm.

Off in the woods, he could hear the whippoorwills crying, "These-old-hills, these-old-hills," as he enjoyed the cool breezes drifting through the open window. Such relaxing, summer evenings were my favorites, as well, when I was privileged to visit my grandparents' mountain home in the late 1940s.

Along about sundown, I recall Grandpa sometimes telling Granny, "I smell Maymer comin' so you oughta fix some supper for him."

Granny could hardly believe Grandpa's sense of smell could be so keen. How could he sniff Maymer's pipe from a mile or so away? It must have been because Grandpa didn't smoke. He might have been able to catch just a faint whiff of strong tobacco on the gentle, summer winds.

So, she rustled back to the kitchen, kindled up a fire, and fixed a quick supper—just in case Grandpa really had smelled that strong pipe. An old mountain saying that comes to mind is "scaring up" some supper. The term probably came from the idea of a really poor mountaineer going out to hunt for a wild animal to prepare for his evening meal.

Over the years it came to be used (in a joking manner) by a lady who hadn't prepared a meal in advance. Granny was usually pretty good at "scaring up" a little supper in a hurry.

Sure enough, in about half an hour, as Grandpa looked off into the evening shadows, he'd announce, "I see Maymer comin' out the trail from the gap of the hill." Granny would hurry to set the hot food on the table.

She liked to feed everybody who came to isolated Bear Mountain. I knew her comment later on would be, "No tellin' how fer the pore man walked to get here. He's prob'ly real hongry." Although she spoke traditional Appalachian English, I always noticed that her archaic words expressed concern for the needs of other people.

After coming so far, the mountain custom was that most guests would "stay all night." Granny kept the big, wooden bed in the loft made up with clean sheets and hand-decorated pillowcases. An elaborately embroidered, matching bedspread covered her pretty patchwork quilts; she was always ready for unexpected company.

After enjoying Granny's good cooking, Maymer would join us in the front room in time to listen to the *Grand Ole Opry*. As darkness settled on peaceful Bear Mountain, Granny lit the kerosene lamps. They cast a soft glow, akin to candlelight, that chased the shadows up to the ten-foot ceiling.

Maymer was a soft-spoken older gentleman, tall, thin, and stoop-shouldered. I thought his name was different and interesting. As Grandpa had been able to detect, he always smoked a pipe packed with burly mountain tobacco. He wore clean, khaki-colored slacks and a matching shirt, so I remember the pipe smoke being strong, but not unpleasant.

Since I was just a little kid, his lifestyle seemed like a mystery to me. Maymer was perhaps what we would describe today as a homeless man, though he surely must have lived somewhere. I wondered if he just roamed the country spending nights here and there with people who knew him. He didn't seem to have a real home like my grandparents.

In retrospect, I have imagined that his neat khakis indicated prior military service; perhaps all Maymer's problems weren't as visible as the bulge on his shoulder blades. Battle Fatigue and Shell Shock in previous wars are now known as Combat Stress Reaction or Post-Traumatic Stress Disorder.

By whatever name, such conditions often contribute to homelessness. Dedicated veterans have served our country honorably in wartime—but many, possibly like Maymer, struggled after their return. Thankfully, the long-term effects of battlefront experiences are better understood now, and more treatments are available.

As the last strains of the *Grand Ole Opry* faded away, I always asked Maymer to play a few songs on Granny's pump organ. He'd act a little shy at first, but he seemed to enjoy playing once he got started.

I was too young for music lessons yet, but I was fascinated with the tall, ornately carved organ in the corner of the living room. It had big mirrors and lots of pretty shelves to display Granny's collection of "what-nots" (a mountain name for small, decorative ornaments. Another common name was simply "purties").

I enjoyed lowering the round, spiral, organ stool so my feet touched the felt-covered pedals. Pumping hard and fast, I carefully and lovingly fingered the yellowed, ivory keys. Granny said the "songs" I played actually had tunes to them.

On these Saturday nights, in the glow of the flickering kerosene lamplight, I watched in amazement as Maymer skillfully played song after song—mostly on the black keys. I thought this must be a special ability and wondered how he was able to avoid nearly all the white keys.

His music filled the living room and sounded so pretty. He played Granny's favorite hymns, especially *Rock of Ages*, and *Amazing Grace*, along with several mountain ballads. We always enjoyed *The Wildwood Flower, The Wreck of Old 97*, and *Barbara Allen.*

When I was finally old enough for piano lessons, I learned (as I had suspected) that playing mostly black keys is quite difficult. The key of F Sharp Major is used for concertos, sonatas, and as least one symphony. Playing in six sharps—the way Maymer did—remains beyond my musical ability to this day.

I still love the squeaky, wheezy reverberation of antique pump organs (that were manufactured in the 1800s). In memory of Granny, I've had my modern, electronic keyboard programmed to duplicate their almost-obsolete musical tones.

Looking back to those Saturday-night visits and recalling the lovely, lost sounds of my childhood, I think of the innate musical ability of a near-homeless man. He obviously had talent. Perhaps in the right environment, he could have become a great musician.

54. *Janie Mae plays the Packard Orchestral pump organ manufactured by Fort Wayne Organ Company, c.1884. It still works, and it is proudly displayed at historic Echo Mountain Inn (built in 1896) in Laurel Park, near Hendersonville, NC.*

I also think about the Southern hospitality and generosity shown by my grandparents. Their welcoming home with plenty of hot food and a soft bed was one of Maymer's regular stops. A relaxing evening on Bear Mountain with an appreciative audience for his music was probably quite therapeutic.

After eating Granny's "scared-up" supper, he could also look forward to a full, country breakfast on Sunday morning. Her specialties included crisp, fat-back bacon and scrambled eggs (freshly gathered from the henhouse). Thick hominy grits were served with sawmill gravy and buttermilk biscuits piping hot from the woodstove. Granny's fluffy biscuits were especially delicious with home-churned butter, blackberry jam, and several cups of scalding coffee.

Maymer always continued on his way after breakfast, but Granny had made sure he was well nourished for wherever the day's journey would take him.

Back then, mountain people welcomed company—even if they could smell them coming two miles away!

Recall your family's hospitality and concern for the less fortunate in the community.

Think about any musical instruments in their home and the people who played them. Share some of their favorite songs with the younger generation (who may not be familiar with old-time tunes—or antique instruments).

Fall Stories

55. Granny and Grandpa would be amazed to see a wild turkey in the home place yard. Not tasty by modern standards, Granny would have figured a way to cook them. She and Grandpa considered mountain wildlife to be God's provision for food.

Fall meant pulling fodder, hulling walnuts, and drying apples

U nlike modern times when fall means a fun daytrip to admire colorful leaves, old-time farm folks had to be diligent during the remaining warm days. Understanding weather signs from years of experience, they knew the harvest had to be gathered "before the ground got all spewed up with frost," as Granny put it.

While Grandpa was at work on the railroad, she worked quickly to cut acres of corn tops and to store the fodder safely in the barn. The coming fall rains could ruin the entire crop after it was already dry. Bushels of corn from those steep, mountainous fields needed to be gathered, shucked, and stockpiled in the four-posted, log corncrib.

The chickens depended on that supply for shelled, crushed corn during the winter, and Granny and Grandpa depended on the chickens for eggs. The cow depended on the fodder, and in turn produced milk and butter.

In fact, everything on the farm was dependent on the fall harvest.

56. Fields of corn are ready to harvest in the fall.
Granny described the annual job as "cutting tops."

Granny and Grandpa also relied on the ancient tree in the yard for a winter's supply of walnuts. However, there was a limited window of opportunity to harvest them, as well.

As the green hulls ripened, they sometimes split and dropped walnuts to the ground. They could also fall with their hulls intact and lie on the ground to soften. However, if fresh walnuts weren't gathered, they would rot quickly during fall rains.

Harvesting them was a job that required more than one pair of gloves to be worn at a time. Juice from soppy hulls could stain the hands for weeks, and was actually potent enough to be used in brown dye. I remember how carefully Granny handled them as she collected the almost ankle-deep walnut harvest in the yard.

Once they were hulled, she spread the walnuts in single layers on pieces of tin in the woodshed. After several weeks, they would dry completely and last through the entire winter.

Walnuts were a good source of natural protein, and farm folks enjoyed cracking them in front of the fireplace during long, winter evenings. I always looked forward to Granny's special walnut cakes during the holidays.

Another time-sensitive task was drying apples, and Granny somehow worked this tasty, winter standby into her schedule. She particularly liked the strange-looking Rusty Coat apples from the oldest tree on the farm. Known to dry quite well, they were medium-sized apples that featured dull red striping overlaid with a darker russet color. Almost unheard of today, this variety had once been very popular in the South, and Granny valued her crooked, aging tree.

Drying apples the old-fashioned way required several steps, all of which depended on good weather. After gathering, washing, coring, and slicing, the apples were arranged in single layers on more big pieces of tin. Granny placed these in the hot sun all day and brought them inside at night.

After a few days, and especially when it rained, she moved the shriveling apple slices to the attic where heat from the tin roof completed the drying process. Carefully storing them in airtight jars to prevent mold, she was ready to make healthy, delicious desserts all winter.

When the busy season was over, Granny felt a great sense of relief, satisfaction, and contentment. Once again, the bountiful harvest had been gathered before cold weather, and she and Grandpa were prepared for the winter ahead.

The old-time trees and the acres of crops are gone now, but considering Granny's rushed fall schedule, it is interesting to realize that multi-tasking isn't a new, modern phenomenon.

Can you recall memories of the busy harvest season at a relative's old-fashioned farm?

Growing and harvesting corn was a mountain necessity

E very fall, Granny harvested the corn crop on the Bear Mountain farm while Grandpa was at work on the railroad. Looking at those hillsides today, the overgrown fields appear to be even more sloping than I remember. Back then, they were used for planting acres of corn to feed both the family and the farm animals.

In fact, growing corn was a tradition that dates to the first settlers in the New World. The kind Indians shared their bounty and taught starving newcomers to plant and harvest the valuable grain. Subsequent generations who pushed westward into the harsh Appalachians were especially grateful for the life-sustaining crop. Like their tough ancestors, Granny and Grandpa maintained a lifelong practice of planting large cornfields.

The versatility of corn made it indispensable on a mountain farm. Although Granny didn't make corncob jelly, the pale, tasty novelty is still sold at mountain tourist attractions. If she'd known about such a possibility, I'm sure she would have made some. Instead, she saved corncobs for quick, fire starters in the cookstove, fireplace, and wood heater.

And she used them to creatively design a corncob doll for me. By tying the cobs together with twine saved from the tops of flour sacks, Granny fashioned the body of the doll. Then, she stuffed its fabric head with cotton, and hand-embroidered the doll's face. Using scraps of colorful, flour-sack fabric, she sewed lovely, detailed clothes, including a bonnet and shoes. In recent years, I donated the doll to the Mountain Heritage Center Museum at Western Carolina University. There, the unusual toy is displayed to demonstrate mountain life, and it is the only corncob doll in the museum. Such a work of art showed Granny's talent and creativity in using free, throw-away items available on the farm. To me, it has been a beloved treasure to keep for posterity.

More uses for the corn crop included "lye hominy" as Granny called it. For the lye, she slowly dripped water through fireplace ashes. As I followed her to the ash barrel beside the Privet hedge, she carefully checked the depth of lye in the drip pan. Then, we went to the corncrib and selected the best ears of dried corn, which Granny carefully shelled. She used the strong, homemade lye and generous amounts of water to boil the corn kernels. When the skins were loosened, she rinsed repeatedly, and finally cooked the fresh, plump hominy. Mountain children considered home-made hominy, generously flavored with butter and salt, to be a treat during long winters. Although I had watched the old-fashioned process, it still seemed somehow magical to me. And I certainly enjoyed Granny's tasty hominy at dinnertime.

When fresh corn ripened in summer, farm families looked forward to boiled "roasting ears" served with butter. In those days, farmhouses didn't have screens, so some folks tossed corncobs out open windows for the free-range chickens. There was a comical story about a large family who enjoyed corn on the cob so much, they ate it by the dozens. Supposedly, anyone who happened to be walking up the road at suppertime could see a "steady stream" of cobs sailing out the kitchen windows as mountain children hungrily ate fresh-boiled corn.

57. On Bear Mountain, fresh corn boils in a large iron pot on an outdoor, wood-fired grill.

Granny didn't need to cook that much corn for a meal, and she wouldn't have thrown cobs out the windows. But in the can house, she reserved several shelves for jars of canned corn to use in cold-weather soups and as an extra vegetable on the table. Corn was one of the most dangerous foods to preserve in Mason jars, but Granny was successful in processing it safely. During stifling summer weather, she kept the woodstove fires burning to boil the filled, canning jars long enough to kill any dangerous bacteria.

Cornbread, of course, was the most common use for the annual crop. Farmers regularly took sacks of corn to the gristmill to be ground into cornmeal. Corn pone (an Indian word) was a mountain staple that Granny served twice a day. There are true stories of folks who ate cornbread at breakfast during hard times. Some learned to like the taste so much, they refused other breads even in better times. Baked in a wood stove with a thick, crunchy crust like Granny's cornbread, it is easy to understand why it remained a lifelong favorite. In modern times, health-food stores sell cornmeal without additives, and I enjoy making cornbread as much like Granny's as possible.

58. Corn muffins and corn on the cob are tasty ingredients at cookouts on Bear Mountain.

Another staple on the farm was fresh-ground grits; folks just didn't think breakfast was complete without them. There was a story from the 1920s about a cute, mountain child who was dotingly asked by a visiting lady, "My goodness, what makes you so purty?" Without hesitation, the three-year-old replied, "Gits and butter." His adorable answer just reinforced the importance of corn on a country farm.

Old-fashioned grits that take a long time to cook are still available today. Admittedly, it takes careful shopping to avoid the instant, quick versions of the mountain favorite. To some degree, Granny's style of food preparation can be replicated in modern times, and I have found it to be a tasty challenge worth pursuing.

Feeding farm animals was an important use for the annual corn crop, as well. Grandpa carefully cracked dried corn kernels to feed the chickens every morning. As I watched from a safe distance, he spread corn by handfuls on the ground in front of the chicken house. To a little kid, it seemed like chickens ran from everywhere pecking, squawking, and flapping toward the bucket as he scooped their breakfast corn.

The barn was always full of dried fodder for the cow, and I remember the fodder supply coming in handy when Grandpa hired a man with a horse to plow the garden. Because Bear Mountain was so remote, the horse stayed in the barn every night for a week during spring plowing. From force of habit, Granny and Grandpa continued raising fields of corn long past their actual need for that much every season. When the barn finally rotted years after Grandpa's death, it was full of fodder. The log corncrib was filled with molded, dried corn when its tall, locust posts eventually toppled over, too.

Mountain people who had once grown corn out of necessity kept growing it from habit. There was a running joke about a farmer with a mule. When asked why he continued to keep the mule when he lived alone on the homestead, he replied, "I need the mule to plow the corn." The next question was, "Why do you still grow so much corn?" The old-timer answered, "I need the corn to feed the mule."

Although the nosy, querying visitor considered the conversation to be a circular line of reasoning, it made perfect sense to the farmer. As it had been for generations, corn was an important, traditional, and versatile crop in the mountains.

Recall anecdotes and stories about your ancestors who grew corn, and remember the tasty corn-based foods on their farm tables throughout the year.

Old-Time Postal Service

U nlike today when we "point and click" to place an online clothing order, Granny walked two miles down Bear Mountain to the Zirconia, NC, Post Office to order a new hat, shoes, or something extra for the house. Folks who lived on the rural route may have hiked even farther to meet the mailman at the nearest state road.

Especially during the Great Depression, postal employees were trained to give extra service to mountain customers. Like shopping at a country grocery store, placing a catalog order was a social event. Aware that the patron may have saved for months to make a special purchase, the postmaster or mailman took time to discuss the merits of the chosen item, to offer information about shipping costs, and to tally the final total.

Their duties included completing Postal Money Orders and assisting with sometimes-confusing Sears-Roebuck order forms. The Item Number might have been listed incorrectly (or on the wrong line) so it was verified from a handy catalog before the envelope was sealed. The entire order was willingly completed if a customer had written a letter to Sears instead of using the catalog form.

59. While still a teenager in 1939, U.S. Postal clerk Virgie Russell responsibly met the train, sometimes twice daily, to receive bags of mail for the Zirconia, NC Post Office.

Those patrons who could not read or write at all were shown even more kindness and consideration. Postal employees were experienced at estimating delivery dates, too, so Granny and other customers wouldn't need to make the long walk again until the package arrived.

On my half-mile walk to the mailbox, I often picked a special apple for the beloved mailman. Then, I eagerly awaited his arrival. Dogs barked, mules brayed, and dust rose as his noisy Model-A clattered and sputtered to a stop at our country mailbox. Ever gracious and smiling, Mr. Osteen declared the misshapen farm apple to be quite beautiful—and just perfect for his lunch.

Old-time postal employees were indeed trained to give extra service to rural customers.

Before electricity, central heat meant wood in the stove

Folks would jokingly estimate, "Why, there must be ten cords of firewood stacked in your yard!" Grandpa just grinned and nodded. He figured there probably was close to that amount—and he liked it that way.

Although Granny and Grandpa never cut a live tree on Bear Mountain, they harvested plenty of dead ones. Their desire for conservation actually made the work more dangerous. Dead timber is even more likely to fall in unpredictable ways and cause serious injury or death.

Before cold weather set in, they would manhandle several trees down the steep mountainside. Heating their house, built in 1895, required a lot of firewood, and Grandpa was well aware of how fast the woodpile could shrink during long snows and ice storms. He felt more secure with a few cords left over at the end of winter.

That an elderly couple could fell so much timber with a two-man, cross-cut saw is nothing short of amazing. Farm ladies in those days certainly had "equal rights." Granny handled her end of the saw as capably as any man.

60. Larry McKinley and Country Hawkins gather and split wood for the coming winter. Notice the antique wheelbarrow and wooden mallet from Country's antique collection.

Once a tree was on the ground, Grandpa would remove any limbs that remained, and hooked an old-fashioned metal peavey to the trunk. Invented back in 1858, this hand tool provided leverage to control the way a log slid down a steep hillside.

To me, it seemed as if time lingered on their mountain a hundred years behind—and my grandparents' woodcutting methods confirmed that idea. Walking, sliding and stumbling behind the bouncing log, they would grasp the wooden handle of the antiquated peavey. This was a tough job, but it enabled Granny and Grandpa to maneuver logs to the house without the aid of a horse or mule.

As a child I "helped" guide some of those logs downhill (at least I thought I was helping). Looking back, I understand why they harvested winter wood from Bear Mountain's tallest ridge. Once wrestled onto the logging road, the tree would actually slide longways down the steep slope. Often, they needed to slow and guide it with the peavey. Gravity was very beneficial, like the antique tool, in bringing whole trees from the forest to the home place.

Farm tractors and chainsaws had been invented at that time, of course, but on Bear Mountain such things were all but unheard of. My grandparents never dreamed of having access to (or even needing) such modern equipment.

In the yard, they continued their work with the two-man saw, cutting the huge log into manageable lengths. Using a heavy maul, Grandpa pounded an iron wedge to make an initial split in each section. Then he spent hours swinging a sharp ax to further slice all those chunks.

When he was satisfied the pieces would fit inside the wood heater, he stacked them to dry. The neat rows were sometimes covered with scrap pieces of tin after they over-flowed the woodshed.

In addition to a large quantity of heater-sized wood, Granny packed the woodshed with smaller sticks for the cookstove. She liked them split long and thin to exactly fit the firebox of her prized 1910-model stove.

In its day, the range was considered to be quite modern. Heavily trimmed in decorative, white enamel, it had several useful features: an overhead warmer, a hot-water reservoir and a handy temperature gauge on the oven door. Unlike our convenient kitchen appliances, however, Granny's stove was operated entirely by wood—lots of wood—every day of the year.

Even in summer, countless stacks of stove wood were needed since Granny baked homemade biscuits every morn-ing. Crusty cornbread and blackberry cobbler were noon-time specialties, along with my seasonal favorites: fried okra and steamed corn-on-the-cob. During those months, too, Granny kept a fire all day while she canned hundreds of quarts of fruits and garden vegetables.

61. Ms. Mandy Gibson, Manager at Historic Johnson Farm in Hendersonville, poses by the 1913 Majestic brand cookstove that was used in the farmhouse. Notice the sticks of wood in the firebox. Cooking three meals a day on a woodstove required a lot of stove wood from the forest.

On weekly ironing days, she also tended the fire for several hours to heat three interchangeable sadirons to quite-high temperatures. Grandpa had always been fastidious, and quite particular, about his clothes. So, she painstakingly pressed distinct creases in heavyweight bib overalls and denim work shirts.

Even red bandana handkerchiefs had to be ironed and folded into neat squares to exactly fit his back pocket. Granny always tried to please Grandpa, and it seemed to please her when he looked good.

A warm, cozy kitchen for all-day ironing was comforting while she watched snow swirling and blowing outside the tall windows. But so much extra heat was overwhelming when the summer sun beamed onto the tin roof. On such hot days, very few breezes stirred through the wide-open doors and windows.

But Granny was a hard worker. She would only stop ironing or canning to bring in more wood (to keep flames leaping inside the cookstove) whatever the outside temperature. During harvest seasons, she continued to talk about the importance of having a good supply of stove wood on hand. Granny recalled that as a young bride, she hadn't known how to plan ahead while Grandpa worked long hours on the railroad. So, during busy harvest times in those early years, she'd also had to gather wood for the cookstove.

In retrospect, I realize that in addition to telling me stories, she was sharing her values of hard work and preparation in life.

Granny liked to reminisce about learning to take advantage of the slackest seasons on the farm. She described watching for pretty days that made it easier to work in the woods.

For cookstove wood, her tools of choice were a bow saw and a chopping ax. Using these, she would cut smaller trees that weren't so far up the mountain. After hacking off the limbs, she could drag those tree trunks to the yard for the final sawing and splitting.

The wooden wheelbarrow came in handy to roll across the fields to the edge of the forest for loads of shorter pieces and chopped-up limbs. Extra effort during the off-season enabled her to gather more kindling and firewood than she would need.

Granny remembered that after adopting the new strategy, she never again ran low on dry split wood during canning time. By planning ahead, she could concentrate on preserving the harvest as fast as it ripened.

She and Grandpa had lived on the mountain a long time. They had come to understand the direct correlation between big stacks of wood and hot fires in the fireplace, wood heater and cookstove.

They didn't think "ten cords" of firewood was too much— and it probably wasn't.

Since electricity wasn't available, central heat really did mean a big pile of wood in the center of the stove—along with more for cooking, baking, ironing and canning.

Do you remember older kinfolks who cooked and heated with wood from a nearby forest?

Think about their work ethic and the old-fashioned tools they may have used. Hopefully, antiques were passed down through the generations—along with memories of full woodbins, sadirons, country cooking and stories around cozy firesides.

Biscuit bread was once a treat in the mountains

An interesting sentence arrangement of archaic Appalachian English was the inclusion of an additional, explanatory word: School house, book learning, Bible book, church house, cooking pan, rifle gun, arm baby, tooth dentist, and cash money are common examples. The same two-word concept was used with foods: ham meat, cow butter, apple fruit, and sweet bread. Yet, cornbread and gingerbread are commonly expressed as one word instead of two.

Biscuit bread, however, was an Appalachian word combination that is both quaint and descriptive. Since wheat was more difficult to grow in the mountains than corn, flour became a prized, purchased commodity from the general store, like sugar and coffee.

During my childhood, Grandpa told a story about a man he knew who had entertained visitors at Sunday dinner. Word had gotten back to the host that the guests hadn't thought much of the meal. Grandpa's friend indignantly declared, "Well, I don't know why they wouldn't have liked it. We had cornbread and biscuit bread, too."

Grandpa understood his friend's exasperation with such picky guests. Back when cornbread was the daily fare, biscuits made any meal special. Mountain people raised corn for cornbread, and some were fortunate to trade extra corn for flour at the gristmill. But buying flour for biscuit bread required cash money, and farmers didn't always have outside incomes.

62. Just like Granny did for many decades, Country Hawkins takes a hot pan of biscuits out of the woodstove oven. He has an electric stove, but he enjoys honoring and maintaining the old ways of his grandparents.

Since he laid crossties on the railroad in addition to farming, Grandpa preferred hearty, homemade biscuits in his lunch bucket. Granny filled them with crisp-fried fatback meat, scrambled eggs, or sometimes peanut butter and jelly. Grandpa always said he couldn't hold out to work on light bread. That Appalachian, two-word description of sandwich bread from the store sounds like it may have originated with some other hard-working fellow. Manual labor required heavier fare than light bread, so it's easy to imagine old-timers' negative opinions of modern, convenience breads. They wouldn't have liked frozen-roll "lumps," and they definitely wouldn't have eaten canned biscuits.

Years before such "gobs of tasteless dough were stuffed into cardboard tubes," Granny's made-from-scratch biscuits stood tall, fluffy, and perfectly browned in the wood cookstove. Because flour was hard to come by, all farm women didn't have experience in baking really good biscuits. But Granny was known to be an expert baker of biscuit bread, and everyone looked forward to the pan coming out of the oven.

Her tasty biscuits couldn't have been described as cathead biscuits, though. That term supposedly came from logging camps where cooks made huge biscuits (comparable to the size of a cat's head). Logging crews were notoriously hungry, and they didn't want dainty tea-biscuits—or normal-sized biscuits, either.

Granny did occasionally bake a big biscuit, commonly called biscuit pone. It was known by that two-word name because of being made like corn pone. A fascinating connection between history and culture is that pone was a Powhatan Indian word documented in the writings of Captain John Smith in the 1600s. As the first settlers gradually pushed westward, the use of pone was retained in traditional Appalachian speech. Granny's pan-sized, biscuit pone was broken or sliced, and I remember it being delicious with fresh-churned butter and her special, wild-huckleberry jam.

One of her baking secrets was using their preferred brand of flour. Martha White flour had been around since 1899, and with added baking powder and salt, it made great biscuit bread. Then, in the early 1950s the new, improved Martha White Self-Rising Flour with Hotrize was highly advertised on the *Grand Ole Opry*. Bluegrass performers,

Lester Flatt and Earl Scruggs, wrote a rhyming song about the new flour, and both the song and the flour are still popular today.

Grandpa would always ask for advertised products when he shopped at Maybin's Grocery in Zirconia, especially 25-lb. bags of his favorite Martha White flour. According to Flatt and Scruggs, its special ingredient, Hotrize, guaranteed that ladies like Granny could bake the very finest biscuits, cakes, and pies. These days, however, Martha White flour is sold in smaller, five-pound bags; we modern cooks just don't bake as much as Granny did.

Another convenience she enjoyed for making biscuit bread was a tall, kitchen cabinet with a built-in flour bin and sifter. Everything necessary for baking was stored in one spacious cupboard, plus it featured a white-enameled, work surface that pulled out for rolling dough.

Granny could sift flour into the biscuit bowl by simply turning a handle. She quickly mixed in baking powder and salt (for plain flour), a hunk of pure lard (or Crisco) and a splash of buttermilk before rolling the dough. Efficiently cutting rounds with an empty, Carnation milk can, she swiftly prepared a long pan of biscuits for the preheated woodstove. This was fast food before it became a modern term. Since Grandpa left before daylight to walk two miles to work, he needed hot breakfast and a take-along lunch shortly after 5 a.m. And Granny always honored the railroad's schedule.

Free-standing kitchen cabinets with handy flour-bin sifters are considered to be antiques today. And when I see them, I think of biscuit bread, chicken and dumplings, and fresh-fruit cobblers. Such a beautiful, wooden cabinet was the first antique that Country Hawkins collected, when he was only 14 years old.

63. Country Hawkins poses with his antique, flour-sifter cabinet that is almost identical to Granny's. In the old days, such a cabinet was considered to be a handy, quite-modern addition to a country kitchen.

He tells the story of visiting his friend's grandmother on her farm. She happened to be in a cleaning mood and was in the barnyard, piling junk onto a bonfire she'd started. She asked the boys to help bring an old cabinet from the shed and toss it into the flames. Even at that young age, Country recognized the quality of the still-usable antique and immediately asked if she'd consider giving it to him. "Well, since I know your grandparents," she said, " you can have it. But I can't imagine why a young boy like you would want such an ugly old thing."

Soon, Country began hand-sanding multiple layers of paint (chipped white, faded yellow, emerald green, and a coat of brown). Finally sandpapering through a tough, gray primer, the industrious young fellow could see the previous beauty of the natural woodgrain.

Encouraged, he removed and soaked the paint-splotched hinges, returning them to their original luster. More antiques followed as Country's expertise grew; now the refurbished cupboard is displayed in his old-fashioned kitchen.

Over four decades ago, the "ugly old thing" narrowly missed being heaped onto a bonfire, but today it is treasured. It is easy to imagine, as Country Hawkins often does, how much biscuit bread has been rolled on the pull-out, enameled work surface. When flour for cobblers and dumplings was a treat, biscuits were for special occasions. Having such a fine, flour-sifter cabinet would have made baking even more enjoyable.

Think about antiques, perhaps in your own family, that were not valued years ago. Hopefully, some of them were saved and are appreciated today.

Ask the oldest person you know if they have memories of homemade biscuits baked in a wood cookstove, especially if flour was hard to come by in that day and time.

Appalachia developed its own unique word combinations—like biscuit bread—that were used by my grandparents. Try to recall regional descriptions of commonplace items in other areas of the United States that may have been a part of your family's heritage. Many such words, their history and meanings, came from other countries and civilizations hundreds of years ago. Because they are distinctive to cultures that are fast disappearing, remembering and sharing them is a way of honoring those who came before us.

In November, folks could sit by the fire and be thankful

By November, fall crops were harvested, and the winter's wood was cut, split, and stacked in the woodshed. Granny and Grandpa finally had time to enjoy long afternoons and evenings sitting by hot, hickory fires in the front room.

During busy planting, hoeing, and gathering seasons, there had been very little time for rest or relaxation. Living off the land—and by the seasons—required long hours, but the rewards came in November when they enjoyed the bounty of the harvest.

Hundreds of quarts of garden fruits and vegetables had been stored in triple rows on can house shelves. Years ago, Grandpa had built the can house by shoveling a three-sided cavity into the hillside. It was sufficiently deep for a person to easily stand, and wide enough for shelves and bins to store a winter's supply of food. A slanted tin roof, the front wall, and a heavy, wooden door completed the structure.

Pumpkins, potatoes, and apples filled the bins, and a crock of homemade kraut sat nearby on the earthen floor. Strings of onions, their dried tops plaited together, hung from the rafters. I remember their pungent, strong aroma that mingled with the musty-earth smell when Granny opened the door.

Being stored almost underground, food didn't freeze even during the coldest winter. If her garden fruits and vegetables had frozen, it would have been a catastrophe—and Granny would have thrown them out. It is interesting that in modern times (because electricity is available) we prefer frozen food. In fact, we think freezing is a perfectly normal method of food preservation.

In the old days, the variety of Granny's home-canned foods reflected the abundance of a good harvest: cherries, beets, beans, corn, okra, tomatoes, cucumber pickles, blackberry jam, and honey with the comb. In the kitchen, strings of dried red peppers and leather-britches beans hung behind the cook stove. There was salt pork in the meat box and plenty of wildlife on the mountain.

Granny and Grandpa knew they had a lot to be thankful for, and their daily attitudes exemplified that spirit of gratefulness. Throughout the year and especially in November, Granny was fond of saying, "We live right well on the mountain."

Modern folks might wonder why she was so grateful since there was no road to their mountain. The nearest highway was a mile through the forest, so their farm was accessible only by narrow footpaths. In that remote section of Henderson County, electricity would not become available until 1975; They lived long lives quite happily without it.

Kerosene lamps served their purposes very well, and food tasted better cooked on the woodstove, anyway. Sitting by a crackling fire in the 1895 rock fireplace, or relaxing around the glowing wood heater, was very comforting on those first cold nights of the season.

The wind always had a special roar across the top of Bear Mountain. I remember cozying up to those hickory fires as night gusts howled; I was snug and warm in my grandparents' simple home.

64. Larry and Janie Mae recreate the preparation of a wood stove to heat a mountain cabin on a cold November evening.

However, I have lived long enough now to realize that their old-time values are rare.

Granny and Grandpa regularly counted the blessings of a winter's supply of wood and a good harvest. Like she always said, "We live right well on the mountain."

Back then, November was a time for countryfolks to sit by the fire and be thankful.

Can you remember warm winter evenings at an older relative's home, and the "attitude of gratitude" that may have been more common back then.

Granny enjoyed baking sweet potato pies in the fall

When leaves on Bear Mountain blazed golden-orange, and morning breezes were invigorated with a noticeable chill, Granny knew it was time to dig the annual sweet potato harvest. Her new-favorite, everyday dessert became sweet potato pie, and she often made several for Sunday dinner.

Her fondness for this seasonal treat brings to mind an old Southern joke that depicted sweet potato pie as the "only" pie worth eating. According to the story, a fellow was traveling beyond Henderson County; perhaps he was making a rare trip to another state to sell produce.

At a restaurant, the server routinely asked if he was interested in dessert. "Yes," he replied, "bring me some pie." He seemed surprised when she inquired, "What kind of pie?" Quite perplexed at her question, he responded, "Why, 'tater pie, lady. What do you think pie is made out of?"

To come to such an adamant conclusion, it seems likely that he'd visited Bear Mountain and eaten Granny's delicious sweet potato pie. It was certainly a favorite of her kinfolks and guests.

Before beginning a tasty baking project, though, Granny needed to carry plenty of stove wood from the woodshed, along with extra buckets of water from the spring. Fortunately, in modern times we don't have those concerns when we decide to bake a pie.

After she "fetched" wood and water, I remember Granny making an extra trip to bring a bucket of sweet potatoes from the can house. She quickly rinsed off most of the garden dirt and dumped the sweet potatoes into a pot of water on the now-glowing wood stove.

Old-timey cooks didn't bother with written recipes, so while the sweet potatoes simmered, Granny gathered her favorite spices for the pies. Next, she sifted several cups of flour and made pie crusts using a hunk of pure lard and a few drops of cold water. Back in those days folks had never heard of frozen, store-bought crusts that come ready-made in flimsy, throw-away pans. When she expertly rolled homemade dough, it always fit the real pie pans perfectly.

Granny demonstrated her trick of dropping cooked sweet potatoes into a pan of spring water to hasten the cooling process and make peeling easier. Then, she mashed the soft, orange pulp with plenty of fresh-churned butter, a handful of white sugar, and maybe a softened lump of brown sugar. As I watched, she whisked several eggs in another bowl with a small can of Carnation milk. Without slowing down, she combined the mixtures, added a spurt of vanilla, and generously sprinkled the entire concoction with nutmeg and cinnamon. Another quick stir, and she folded it all into unbaked pie crusts.

Sliding the pans into the oven, she added occasional sticks of wood to the firebox to keep the temperature as close to 375 degrees as possible. Her 1910-model stove featured a thermometer built into the oven door, so with careful tending of the fire, she could maintain a fairly constant temperature. Forty years' experience using that same stove showed in the quality and flavor of her cooking. Spicy aromas began filling the house, and Granny's pies came out perfectly browned on the edges and firm in the center. That would be an accomplishment using a modern electric stove and was doubly so in a wood-fired oven.

65. *Our neighbor, Ardie Gallant, poses with a homemade sweet potato pie on Bear Mountain. This old-fashioned, Southern treat is reminiscent of the fall seasons when Granny baked similar pies here on the mountain.*

As I contentedly played with my favorite rag dolls on the warm kitchen floor, I looked forward to the first slice of fresh, homemade pie. It is interesting to recall that I never cared for Granny's eight-layer, stacked pumpkin pies. But I loved sweet-potato pies. Maybe she sometimes stacked them together, but I remember individual crusts that stayed nice and crisp. Granny was fond of the thin, softened layers in her stacked pies, but I preferred thicker, cinnamon-laced filling on a crunchy crust. To my 7-year-old taste, sweet potatoes were more flavorful than pumpkins, anyway, so I eagerly anticipated Granny's fall-time pies coming out of the oven.

In addition to flavor, country ladies planned these seasonal menus by necessity since old-timers like Granny and Grandpa grew most of their own food. Even as a child I knew the rocky fields on beautiful Bear Mountain were not ideally suited for raising crops. But I also knew that Granny's annual garden was prolific. I balanced those two opposites by attributing her success to hard work. I could see mounds of rocks she'd carried by the bucketful to the ends of garden rows, but there were lots more in those fields.

Still, one crop that grew relatively well in poor, rocky soil was sweet potatoes. And every fall, Granny harvested several long rows. Admittedly, most were misshapen by today's standards, but mashed into pies, no one knew the difference. Hard rocky soil prevented sweet potatoes from attaining the perfect-oblong "football" shape—but they stubbornly continued to grow. Tough mountaineers could appreciate the resilience of the sweet potato to adapt to a less-than-desirable environment. Folks like Granny and Grandpa had a lot in common with this determined plant. They came from a hearty stock of Welsh-Scotch-Irish ancestors who had survived in these rugged mountains for generations.

Still, Granny would be thrilled and amazed at the beautifully shaped sweet potatoes routinely displayed in produce sections of modern grocers. Most of these are grown in the more-suitable soil and hotter weather of Eastern North Carolina. In fact, over 40 percent of sweet potatoes produced in the entire United States come from North Carolina, making our state number one in production. No wonder the humble sweet potato has been adopted as the Official State Vegetable. Although in competition with other practical suggestions like corn and collard greens, the versatile, tasty, and marketable sweet potato was chosen.

66. Along with fresh apples and vegetables, Henderson's Farms on Tracy Grove Road sells a lot of sweet potatoes every fall. Local customers appreciate the healthful flavor so much that bins this size are emptied and refilled several times during the season.

After all, it has been around a long time. Thought to have been cultivated in Peru maybe 3,000 years ago, the sweet potato became a South American staple and was eventually carried to the Caribbean islands. It was there that Christopher Columbus found delicious sweet potatoes and took some back to Spain. Relished by Europeans despite their less-than-ideal growing seasons, the tasty, durable root was among the provisions brought to Virginia by English settlers in the 1600s. However, Native Americans who lived farther south were already growing sweet potatoes when Hernando de Soto explored their area (circa 1540). Somehow the healthful sweet potato had been transported, perhaps through Central America and Mexico, to those more-southern cultures.

Centuries later, our Thanksgiving dinners wouldn't seem like a celebration without sweet potato casserole. And I'm probably not the only Southerner who prefers sweet potato pie to pumpkin pie. More uses, even today, are being found for this versatile, vitamin-packed root. In recent times, bags of sweet potato chips are displayed along with regular potato chips. Some restaurants offer sweet potato fries in place of regular fries, and a roasted sweet potato can often be substituted for a steak-house, baked potato.

It seems that the more we learn about the ancient sweet potato, the more we want to incorporate it into our diet. Nutritionists now realize it is one of the highest foods in beta carotene, Vitamins A, B6, C, D, iron, manganese, and fiber. As Granny would say, "A sweet 'tater is good for all that ails you." In addition to pies, she sometimes fried thick slices in butter, and she often baked them. Mountain stories recall children carrying hot, baked sweet potatoes in their pockets on snowy walks to school. This handy, take-along lunch also kept their hands warm.

Think about creative ways your ancestors used this annual fall crop. Recall your favorite recipes—along with tasty sweet potato pies.

Thanksgiving pumpkin pies were stacked eight layers high

Traditionally, mountain people didn't serve turkey and cranberry sauce at Thanksgiving. The annual day of thanks was more commonly celebrated with wild game from the woods, pork or chicken from the farm, preserved garden vegetables—and homemade pumpkin pie.

Like my grandparents, most countryfolks felt blessed to live on self-sufficient farms in the North Carolina mountains. They were thankful for the bounty of the harvest, and few saw the need of serving "store-bought" foods at holidays.

Granny never missed an opportunity to load her long table with home-grown specialties, and country-fried cabbage was one of Grandpa's year-round favorites.

After she made a crock of kraut for the winter, the remaining summer cabbages were preserved fresh in the garden. Granny prepared long trenches lined with fall leaves, turned each cabbage upside down and buried it with more leaves on top. Then she heaped garden dirt around the mounds so only a few cabbage roots showed.

Before electricity became available, older mountain folks understood ways of preserving farm produce, and they grew almost everything they needed for winter.

When Grandpa had a craving for fried cabbage, Granny went to the garden and pulled up a crisp, fresh head. The outer leaves might have turned dark, but the inside layers were white, tender, and tasty.

Using a homemade "food processor" (a Carnation evaporated-milk can with the top removed) Granny soon had the large cabbage diced; Then, she quickly steamed it (with a few drops of water) in sizzling, fatback grease.

Fried cabbage was as welcome at holiday meals as it was any other time. Granny liked to serve it with home-canned green beans, corn, and pickled beets from the can-house shelves. She regularly made her original gravy-potatoes, which I thought were delicious with crumbled cornbread. Jars of blackberry jam and honey with the comb were on the table, too, since Grandpa wanted them handy for buttered, hot biscuits.

A few older kinfolks and neighbors still have fond memories of Granny's country cooking—and nobody could forget her eight-layer pumpkin pie at Thanksgiving and for Sunday dessert.

The extensive preparation for this edible work of art gave her a lot of enjoyment. She retrieved a pumpkin from the can house, removed the seeds, cut it in chunks, and peeled each piece. Next, she steamed the pumpkin slices until they were tender.

After mixing spices, eggs, sugar, and milk into the drained pumpkin, she was ready to make eight identical pie crusts. To modern cooks like us, that might be a problem.

However, in Granny's experienced hands, pie-crust dough stayed together, rolled out perfectly, and easily transferred to all eight pie pans. Then, she carefully ladled a thin layer of pumpkin filling into each identical crust and baked them a few at a time in the woodstove.

67. Eight-layer pumpkin pies were one of Granny's homemade, holiday specialties.

I remember the aroma of savory spices filling the kitchen when she opened the oven door.

After the thin pies cooled, Granny artfully stacked them all on one large plate, each on top of the other—eight layers tall. The pie was then sliced like a cake, and guests marveled at her masterpiece.

An eight-layer pumpkin pie, towering above all the other foods on Granny's Thanksgiving table, was quite special.

She had learned to use ordinary cabbages, potatoes, pumpkins (whatever was available on the farm) to make tasty dishes—and her favorite saying was, "We live right well on the mountain."

Country creativity, mixed with gratefulness, was a good combination for an old-fashioned Thanksgiving.

Think about holiday specialties at an older relative's home, especially if the unique recipes featured foods grown on the farm.

Any Time Stories

68. The 1912 mantle clock cost $1.25, and it still worked (somewhat) in the 21ˢᵗ century when Janie Mae donated it to the Mountain Heritage Center Museum on the campus of Western Carolina University.

Telling time by the mantle clock or by looking at the sun

W hen Granny worked in the fields, I remember her look-ing up at the sun and saying, "We'd better get started back to the house. It's about a quarter to four, and I need to build a fire in the cookstove. I want to have Grandpa's sup-per ready when he gets home." At the house, a few minutes later, I was amazed to look at the mantle clock and see it approaching 4:00 p.m., just like she said.

Granny's ability to determine not only the hour, but the minutes, came from farming on Bear Mountain so many years. In those days farm families lived close to the earth. They were aware of changing seasons and were familiar with the sun's horizontal angle across the mountains. Granny learned to carefully observe the position of the sun for a very practical reason. She couldn't keep running back to the house and looking at the clock to see what time to start supper.

As part of daily farm chores, Granny milked in the barn, worked in the fields, boiled laundry at the wash place, and gathered eggs in the chicken house. She carried water from the spring, fed the pigs, or cut wood in the forest. So, she was away from the front-room clock for most of every day. Granny was close enough to the house to hear the clock's hourly clangs when she was hanging wet laundry on the clothesline, or if she was working in her flower garden. However, most daily chores required her to be much farther from the front yard.

But she would never risk wearing her treasured necklace-watch while she worked in the fields. It's round, gold pendant featured a little cover that opened to reveal a lovely ladies' watch (that kept perfect time). Granny saved such a decorative keepsake to wear with Sunday clothes since it looked more like good jewelry than a timepiece. In fact, the watch was so special, Granny would sometimes take it out of the chifforobe and show me how she carefully wound it. I never did know if the necklace had been a gift, or if she bought it for herself. But I noticed that Granny handled her beautiful pendant-watch with extraordinary care. No wonder she learned to depend on the position of the sun to know when to leave the field during work days.

And she needed to stay on time to please Grandpa. It seemed to me that he must have learned his life habits from observing railroad schedules. Southern Railway prided itself with keeping trains running on time. And I'm sure that trackmen like Grandpa were instructed to work quickly before the next train was due.

Years later when Grandpa retired, one of his favorite activities was listening for the high-pitched, reverberating whistle of the early-evening train. After supper, he'd sit by the high steps, put in a "chaw" of home-grown tobacco, and periodically check his reliable railroad watch. When the steam-powered train finally chugged around the bend about a mile down the mountain, Grandpa would sometimes declare, "Ole 630 is runnin' two minutes late tonight."

Like Granny, he treasured his personal timepiece. Railroad men appreciated having an authentic railroad watch, and his remained accurate as long as he lived. He proudly carried the valuable watch, secured with a thick, gold chain, in the front pocket of his bib overalls. For decades, it kept him on time during the two-and-a-half-mile hike to work every morning. Being late for work, being late for supper, or being late for anything, didn't suit Grandpa.

Even after retirement, he wanted a strict, daily schedule. And being a dutiful woman of her generation, Granny always honored what Grandpa wanted. Their day began at 4:00 a.m., just as it did during his working years. A home-cooked breakfast was prepared on the woodstove and eaten early so Grandpa could listen to the 6:00 morning news and weather on the battery radio.

Lunch (known as "dinner" back then) was the biggest meal of the day, and it was served at exactly 11:00 a.m. That didn't mean five minutes past eleven (or even worse, ten minutes later). Granny went to the garden or can house early, so she could cook Grandpa's food on time. Then, she prepared a light supper to be eaten at exactly 4:00 p.m. They went to bed at 8:00 in the evening, even if it was still daylight outside.

The clangs of the 1912 mantle clock kept Granny and Grandpa on schedule when they were in the house to hear them. Of course, most folks in the mid-1950s used electric clocks, but my grandparents considered the wind-up mantle clock to be more dependable. Grandpa liked to point out that it worked even when modern, electrical service was disrupted by snowstorms.

The mantle clock had been quite expensive in its day. Grandpa paid $1.25 for it back in 1912, when he earned ten cents per hour on the railroad. That was quite an investment, but it never failed to keep time all those decades.

On Sunday nights, I remember Grandpa carefully winding the clock with its special key. This simple maintenance kept it running for a whole week—sounding once on the half hour and announcing each hour with the appropriate number of clangs—throughout the morning, at noon, as evening shadows crept into the front room, and all night, as time passed by the measured tick of the wind-up, mantle clock.

It has been thought-provoking for me to envision the constancy of the 1912 clock. When frightening and horrifying events were taking place in other parts of the world, the clock kept responding, tick-tock, tick-tock, on peaceful Bear Mountain.

It sounded out the hours when World War One began and ended. It was ticking the day the stock market crashed in 1929. It kept time during the long days of the Great Depression, clanged while Pearl Harbor was being bombed in 1941, and kept on ticking throughout the years of World War Two. When times got better, it still rang out the hours, unfailingly, regularly, and accurately on remote Bear Mountain.

Looking at the grown-over farm today, it might be difficult to realize the importance of listening for the clang of the mantle clock or the need to observe the sun as a timepiece. Yet, these methods were vital when Granny gathered crops in the fields. During the decades Grandpa worked on the railroad, she needed to balance daily farm responsibilities with the need of timely meal preparation.

Even if her personal timepiece hadn't been a dressy necklace, few other watches could have been worn to hoe corn, cut wood, or boil clothes in the iron wash pot. Most would have been ruined after just a few days. Learning to tell time by looking at the sun was an efficient way to stay on schedule on a mountain farm.

And in modern times, it is a skill that few of us would have. Perhaps you have heard similar stories about your ancestors' abilities. You may remember a special grandfather clock, cuckoo clock, pocket watch, or other old-fashioned timepieces at your grandparents' home. Be sure to share those memories with younger generations who might not understand the significance of a simple, wind-up clock.

Mountain people spoke
Old English in a New World

As a child in Henderson County in the late 1940s and early 1950s, I was privileged to be a part of two worlds: the old and the new. At Tuxedo Elementary School, students received instruction at a level comparable with many private schools.

69. Mr. Dean A. Ward (1904-1991) principal and teacher at Tuxedo Elementary School 1941-1968.

Principal and teacher Dean Ward was capable and dedicated, and many of his pupils later earned advanced degrees in medicine, law, education, and business. Most of the country children succeeded and made good lives for themselves, and some even became millionaire entrepreneurs.

To this day, I think of Mr. Ward when I see incorrect English on signs: 20 items or less; Sprinklers come on automatic, etc. He stressed correctness, so we were taught the difference between less and fewer, and when to use adverbs. Back then, Mr. Ward was over-qualified for a country schoolteacher, but we certainly benefited from his master's degree in English.

In contrast, I visited my beloved grandparents' mountain home during weekends. There, I heard Appalachian English words and expressions—which were quite different from "proper" English. Looking back, it seems that I would have had trouble adjusting to such different worlds.

Perhaps it seemed more natural because I held Granny and Grandpa in almost reverential awe and respect and looked forward to visits. He had recently retired from Southern Railway after forty years of service, and by mountain standards he and Granny lived a good life. They continued to farm, and Granny enjoyed sewing, crocheting, and cooking big meals for company.

Even though I could recognize misplaced pronouns and double negatives, I instinctively understood their archaic terms to be part of a real language—their native language. I eventually learned that much of Appalachian English (also known as Old English) came from wide-ranging areas of Great Britain with some words from Germany.

There seemed to be a certain amount of authenticity when Grandpa said "holp" as a past tense of help: "I holp him stack the wood."

"Heered" was used for heard, "ax" for ask, "tote" for carry, and "fetch" for bring. To "bile" was to boil, and a "peckerwood" was a woodpecker. Since it was two miles to the store, they reckoned, "Hit's a right smart piece."

A "waist" was a blouse that needed to be "warshed" (washed). A "gaum" was disorderly clutter, and Granny particularly disliked the "loft" (attic) to be in a "gaum." Someone who "bummed" on her pump organ played a series of discordant notes (instead of a song).

Decades later, I was thrilled to come upon the research of Dr. Michael B. Montgomery, Professor of English and Linguistics at the University of South Carolina. Now retired, this Knoxville, TN, native has written extensively about the use of English in Appalachia. In addition to his comprehensive (710-page) *Dictionary of Smoky Mountain English,* his numerous articles include *Exploring the Roots of Appalachian English*, and *The Pace of Change in Appalachian English.*

Similar research has stressed the importance of preserving colloquial words in other cultures. Both the *Dictionary of Newfoundland English* and the *Dictionary of Alaskan English* have been compared with Dr. Montgomery's studies in his native Appalachian Mountains.

His work is especially interesting, because it reminds me of hearing those same lyrical words spoken by my grandparents. I have so appreciated learning about ancestral heritage, and it is fascinating to ponder how the archaic vocabulary filtered down to the 20th century.

When immigrants first came to the New World, they brought their language and colloquial sayings. Expressions that seem antiquated now were once a part of daily conversation in the various parts of Great Britain. Those folks left in large numbers in search of land and a better life in the New World. Although it was usually a generation or two before they pushed west into the Blue Ridge Mountains, portions of their language endured.

Because of stagecoach roads there was some contact with the outside world by the late 1700s, but the people of Appalachia saw theirs as a distinct community within itself.

To some extent, they chose to be isolated by remaining at their generational home places.

In eras of war and economic depression, there was more security on self-sustaining farms than was available to the masses of the poor who lived in cities. The ability to grow food on their own land provided family stability in uncertain times.

Surrounded by extended relatives, mountain folks farmed the steep hillsides as their parents before them. Each generation seemed to feel a deeper and more-meaningful sense of place in these ruggedly beautiful mountains. Tourists arrived early in the 1800s, and still come today, looking for the same peaceful solitude that mountain people grew up on.

Hard-working folks born in western North Carolina adapted to farm life and were grateful for land ownership. Many in the 1800s, including Granny and Grandpa, had been deprived of the opportunity for "book learnin'" (formal education). Understanding that times were changing, my grandparents highly valued education for "young folks."

During childhood, I was in the unique position of learning the new (at an exceptional elementary school) while appreciating the old (on Bear Mountain).

Recalling the charm of their colloquial words, I like to imagine that Old (Appalachian) English still has a cadence reminiscent of the rhythms of Irish fiddle music. If we listen closely, we can possibly hear a faint echo of Scottish bagpipes. Perhaps phrases from a tragic English ballad survived in the melodious dialect of our forefathers.

Well into the 20th century, mountain speech included colorful and quite-descriptive conversational terms that were once common throughout the British Isles.

When visiting the sick, Granny described an older lady as "right peart" (if the woman was recovering).

How fondly I recall my great-aunt inviting me to "Stay as long as you can. It's right airish out there."

In summer, "young'uns" (children) were cautioned to watch out for "waspeas" (wasps).

If unexpected company arrived, Granny hurried to set hot food on the table and explained, "No tellin' how fer the pore man walked to get here. He's prob'ly real hongry."

Even as a small child, I observed that much of their quaint conversation centered around their genuine concern and care for others. Perhaps you, too, were privileged to grow up with such good-hearted people and to hear at least a few old words and expressions.

Your family may have lived in a different part of the United States, but colloquialisms from their countries of origin could have been retained for a few generations. It might be interesting to share any that come to mind.

Stories we heard as children, conversations we recall, or perhaps old letters, include the very words of our beloved ancestors. Their Old-World language is a vibrant part of our heritage, and as Granny would say, "It'd be a pity to lose it."

Mountain ladies like Granny always wore aprons

The first thing a country woman did when somebody knocked on the door was to take off her apron (unless it was freshly ironed). A proper lady wouldn't think about answering the door wearing an apron that might have kitchen stains.

When someone was making pictures, it was unusual that Granny didn't remove her apron just as quickly. So, finding a vintage photo of Granny wearing one of her homemade, flour-sack aprons is a treasure. Aprons served the practical purpose of protecting good housedresses from everyday spills, soot from the woodstove, splashes of frying-pan grease, or dirty dishwater. Therefore, they weren't suitable to be worn in in a photograph and certainly not in front of unexpected guests.

There are stories about mountain ladies using two aprons, so they were always wearing a clean one to serve a meal after it was cooked. I don't know that Granny ever thought of that idea, but it would have been a great way to impress guests. They wouldn't have known about the discarded apron that had been hastily stuffed behind the woodbin. Wearing the fresh-pressed apron, Granny could have ushered folks to the overflowing table as though the food had magically appeared.

70. A rare photograph of Granny wearing a flour-sack-fabric apron on Bear Mountain.

For mountain ladies like Granny, a soiled apron was comparable to a dirty dishcloth. Like those everyday "dishrags" it was inevitable that aprons would become stained—but they could never be seen by guests. So on occasion, I do remember her mad dash to the bedroom to change aprons just before company arrived.

There were several designs for aprons, but Granny favored a below-the-knee style. It featured a high-bibbed front with wide shoulder pieces that joined to form a circle behind her neck. The apron was secured by tying a pretty bow in the back with a wide, sewn-in sash.

As a child, it seemed to me that Granny's aprons were almost like wrap-style dresses that completely covered her clothes. Because she boiled laundry in the iron wash pot and rinsed it underneath the waterspout at the wash place, wearing flour-sack aprons reduced the need to launder heavy dresses so often. And she could always flip the apron off and look presentable in her clean housedress if unexpected company arrived.

Before Grandpa's retirement from the railroad, he purchased flour in large, economical 50-lb. bags. Various family members lived with them at times, plus he carried several biscuits in his lunch bucket every day. Those bigger sacks provided more printed fabric for Granny's sewing projects, including full-length aprons. When my grandparents lived alone on the mountain, they switched to 25-lb. bags of flour. Cotton cloth from those smaller bags could be cut and pieced. Granny liked to use the free fabric to design aprons, kitchen curtains, quilts, and doll clothes.

During the years of the Great Depression, flour companies competed to print the prettiest patterns on the cotton sacks. They knew ladies would save matching flour bags to accumulate enough cloth for a dress or a complete set of curtains. That meant the family would continue buying the same kind of flour and develop brand loyalty. Each company's goal was to produce the most striking designs, so more than 20,000 different flour-sack patterns were eventually manufactured.

Granny used a lot of them over the years and was glad to have free fabric. Almost any design on flour sacks suited her, and this black-and-white photo shows the intricate print on her apron. Although she sewed it for the practical purpose of keeping her housedress clean, it is fun to imagine the colors.

Maybe the fabric was a combination of red diamond-design shapes interspersed with yellow-diamond shapes on a pastel blue background. Flour-sack prints tended to be showy and eye-catching to attract attention to their brand of flour. So, it is likely that the colors on Granny's apron were quite bright.

Like most of the other clothes boiled in the iron wash pot, Granny painstakingly starched and ironed flour-sack aprons. They eventually became stained, but she was quite particular about starting her workday fresh and nice. Besides keeping her dress clean, Granny found many other uses for colorful aprons.

She gathered the last apples from the tree and carried them in her upturned apron. Sometimes, there just weren't enough to make a trip to the barn to "fetch" a feed bucket. Likewise, she could carry a few onions, potatoes, or ears of corn for supper. Then, she could bring in a few extra pieces of kindling for the cookstove.

Flapping her apron at a chicken she was chasing, or waving it to shoo away bumblebees were other practical uses. A folded apron end was a great emergency potholder if a pan was boiling over. And Granny's upturned apron would hold most of the eggs from the henhouse on a given day. Sometimes an overworked farmwife could catch a few winks while leaning back in a porch rocker. To rest without the interruption of flies buzzing around her face, she could flip her handy apron over her head.

Historically, aprons were more popular during times when homes and keeping house were honored as life goals for women. A lady wearing an apron seemed to be warm and caring about her home and family. She just looked hospitable—like fresh biscuits or warm gingerbread would be ready at a moment's notice. As women entered the workforce, they discarded aprons because they weren't in the kitchen all day like ladies in their grandmothers' era.

Modern, food-themed television shows, however, have brought a resurgence of apron wearing. Learning to bake bread from scratch or trying new, complicated recipes reveal the practicality of covering good clothes. Our great-grandmothers would be pleased, and perhaps a little amused, that we are relearning things they already knew.

Aprons were once so common they were referenced in an old-timey slur. It was particularly insulting if the person being discussed happened to be a local man. "Gossipy ole ladies" would declare, "You know he'll never amount to anything, 'cause he'll always be tied to his Mama's apron strings!" Their derision indicated the fellow was incapable of making ordinary adult decisions without first seeking his mother's advice, permission, or approval.

Likewise, an up-and-coming young man might be warned away from an overly dependent girl who refused to leave her mother's side. He would be told he'd have to "marry the whole family" because "she'll always be tied to her Mama's apron strings."

In modern times, that warning is a figure of speech, but in the days when aprons were a common part of women's attire, people could easily visualize its implications. Perhaps the saying originated decades earlier when country children in isolated areas weren't used to visitors. When guests arrived, the children would timidly crowd around their mother. They would actually "hide" underneath her apron until they felt comfortable with the new folks. Back then, such shyness was socially acceptable for a small child, but the derisive figure of speech inferred that not much had changed when they became adults.

Old-fashioned aprons were more than pieces of colorful, flour-sack fabric. They represented safety for a small child and home to the entire family. Additionally, they served as vegetable, fruit, and egg carriers, as well as emergency pot holders.

Recall aprons your grandmother wore and the sense of warmth and hospitality they engendered in her guests—including good food simmering on her cookstove. Were you familiar with homemade aprons sewed from flour sacks? Think about the many designs and bright colors of flour-sack fabric that you remember.

The Interesting History of Flour Sacks

U nlike today's small paper bags, flour was shipped in large wooden barrels in the 1800s. Before frozen rolls, refrigerated biscuits, baking mixes, or commercially baked bread, flour was sold in large quantities. Ladies needed much bigger sizes than we see in modern stores, since they baked homemade bread three times a day (along with cakes, dumplings, fruit cobblers, and pies).

Large cotton sacks gradually replaced the heavy barrels by the 1890s, and frugal housewives began recycling them into sewing fabric. However, the brand-label imprint was so difficult to remove they resorted to soaking the entire bag in kerosene. This procedure was only partially successful, but ladies continued using the blotched, free cloth in an era of "use it up, wear it out, make it do, or do without."

In the 1920s the popularity of the new synthetic fabric, rayon, caused the price of cotton to drop drastically. Realizing a cost savings, companies quickly expanded the use of cotton material for 25-lb. and 50-lb. feed and flour sacks. Surprisingly, they were slow to realize the marketing possibilities of decorative designs.

71. Authentic and colorful flour-sack fabric like
Granny used is displayed on Bear Mountain.

However, by 1925, colorful prints were introduced along with easily removed paper labels. During the Great Depression, home sewing was essential for many families, so housewives who didn't particularly like a brand of flour continued to buy it if the fabric bags had the prettiest designs. To accumulate enough matching cloth to sew a new dress or a complete set of curtains, customers developed brand loyalty.

Then, each flour company attempted to create the prettiest prints (especially of multicolored flowers) hoping to retain customers in the slow economy. Over the years, 20,000 different designs were manufactured, each more intricate, vibrant, and detailed than the last.

During World War II, women were encouraged to show patriotism and help the war effort by recycling flour and feed sacks into clothing. In our North Carolina mountains, the popularity of this colorful, free fabric continued through the 1950s.

Like other ladies of her era, Granny found multiple uses for the pretty flour sacks. Some of her favorite projects included ruffled kitchen curtains (starched and ironed to perfection), She also pieced quilts, made everyday aprons and dresses for herself, and sewed lovely clothes for the rag and corncob dolls she designed for me.

On a rural farm, flour and feed sacks were easily repurposed to store seeds, to carry mail, groceries, or books. They were useful to strain milk and cover milk jugs—or to stuff a crack to keep out winter drafts. The versatile, free fabric was utilized to sew baby and doll clothes, dresses, underwear, nightgowns, and aprons. It could be hemmed for use as diapers and head scarves.

Country ladies always used flour sacks for cleaning and dusting, and in the days before electricity, the soft cotton cloth was especially helpful to polish the glass globes of kerosene lamps.

Creative housewives braided flour-sack rugs to display in the living room, and sewed quilts, sheets and pillowcases to use in the bedroom. For the kitchen, they designed curtains, made tablecloths. dish towels and potholders. Then, they made good use of any remaining fabric as a convenient cover for leftover breakfast biscuits.

Times have changed.

Now, flour is sold in two-pound or four-pound size paper bags. Modern ladies prefer refrigerated biscuits in cardboard tubes, or (even faster) bacon-egg-cheese biscuits at a drive-thru. The very idea of 50-lb. sacks of flour would seem overwhelming—and the prospect of sewing a dress from the fabric bags would be just as daunting.

In fact, colorful, printed flour sacks are now so rare that vintage clothing and quilt seamstresses pay as much as $40.00 each if they can find antique bags in good condition.

Who would have dreamed that cotton flour sacks—so common and useful in our grandmothers' lifetimes—would become collectors' items?

Country men wore bib overalls for comfort and practicality

Hard-working men like Grandpa preferred old-fashioned bib overalls instead of work pants, blue jeans, or slacks. They liked the comfort and the convenience of a one-piece garment that was worn loosely without a constricting belt. Along with providing added protection for the shirtfront, the bib featured extra pockets for watches, pencils, pipes, and pipe tobacco.

A matching overall jacket and blue-serge shirt completed the workingman's outfit. Men wearing that style of clothing were common in Appalachia into the 1950s, and some still follow the tradition today.

Overalls have a long history, at least to the 1850s, so they have been around for more than 150 years. The name originally indicated that overalls were meant to be worn "over all" to protect other clothes. In time, the one-piece design developed into a comfortable clothing style favored by carpenters, railroad workers, and farmers.

Smaller-sized overalls, also with matching denim jackets, were marketed by promoting the idea of a young boy becoming "Dad's helper." In reality, overalls were the sturdiest clothes available, as well as the most economical for both men and boys. Early Sears-Roebuck catalogs show the cost of men's overalls and jackets at 75 cents each. However, by 1923, the price increased to $1.69 for each garment. Matching overalls and jackets for boys were 95 cents each in the same catalog.

House painters tended to prefer white overalls, and some carpenters wore gray-and-white striped, but dark-blue denim was the most popular color for working men like Grandpa. The darker the blue denim, the newer the garment, and country men and boys liked new-looking overalls. Faded denim indicated the overalls were worn, thin, and old, and wearing such washed-out clothes implied that a family couldn't afford anything better.

It's probably just as well that Grandpa didn't live to see the modern, teenage fad of wearing "distressed" denim jeans. He would certainly have been "distressed" and unable to understand such fashions. In fact, when the style first became popular, country men told store clerks they already had jeans that looked like the faded denim on display. They explained that they had come to town especially to buy new clothes, and they wanted traditional, dark-blue denim—so they looked new.

And Grandpa certainly could not have comprehended the idea of buying expensive, name-brand jeans that had been purposely ripped and shredded at the factory. In his day, faded, torn, or threadbare clothes were a sure sign of poverty. Country women like Granny diligently saved worn-out overalls and cut them up to use as discreet, strengthening patches to make newer overalls last longer. Mothers of small boys certainly patched a lot of overall knees that were worn from kneeling in the dirt to shoot marbles, plant gardens, and explore hillsides. Mountain folks didn't want to look "poor" even though they lived on farms, worked as laborers, and wore old-timey, practical, inexpensive overalls.

72. Grandpa (right) and his brother, Uncle Boney, wore bib overalls, blue-serge shirts, and overall jackets all their lives. Their chosen attire was comfortable, practical, and economical for farming and working as railroad trackmen.

During the Great Depression, growing boys felt themselves fortunate to have new overalls when school started in the fall. A "big" Christmas was when they received two pairs, and passed outgrown overalls to a younger brother. Clothes might not be purchased again until farm crops were sold the next fall. Over the summer, country children's overalls sometimes became worn to the point of resembling chaps.

There are stories about boys in such circumstances determining in their own minds to work hard and buy really nice clothes when they grew up. Rather than being a reason to lose hope, such faded, outgrown overalls inspired country boys to improve their lot in life.

This was true to some extent in Grandpa's life, as well. Mindful of his appearance, Grandpa was quite particular about shirts, overalls, and jackets being as new as he could afford. Having grown up helping in his mother's laundry business, he was used to clean, ironed clothes. So, Grandpa wanted his work clothes freshly laundered and pressed. Using sadirons heated on the woodstove, Granny ironed distinct creases in the legs and sleeves, and she was always proud when Grandpa looked good.

Along with a strong work ethic (also from his mother) Grandpa's neat appearance likely helped when he was selected for a supervisory position at the railroad. Lacking confidence in his self-taught education, he turned down the opportunity. But the offer showed that common workmen, who took pride in the way they wore old-fashioned bib overalls`, could advance on the job. Grandpa used the principles of "dressing for success" long before books were published on the subject.

An interesting concept about the history of sturdy, denim overalls and jeans is that they were developed during the 1849 gold rush. At age 24, Levi Strauss arrived in California with a supply of canvas to sell for tents and wagon covers. When the young entrepreneur learned that tough work clothes were more in demand, he experimented with sewing "waist overalls" from the canvas. Discovering that it was too stiff, he switched to a twill fabric.

Over time, the jeans-type pants he designed became more popular with some men than the protective-bib overalls. Working men of both persuasions were pleased when Strauss continued developing stronger clothes by adding metal rivets to the stress points of the pockets.

The blue jeans we are familiar with today evolved from those gold-rush-era experiments. The popularity of wearing them was further advanced when western movies were commercialized. Youngsters wanted to dress like their favorite cowboy, so sales of blue jeans increased nationwide.

Of course, Grandpa and other mountain fellows didn't care what cowboys wore, so they continued to favor more-comfortable bib overalls. Some men still wear them to church (sometimes with a white shirt) and serve as ushers every Sunday. In fact, the tradition is so much a part of Appalachian culture that brides have chosen overalls for groomsmen in otherwise-formal weddings. And the photos were beautiful with the bride and bridesmaids in long gowns while the men honored their heritage by wearing bib overalls.

Western-themed weddings in decorated, event barns are quite popular these days. To match the décor, groomsmen are dressed in blue jeans. And they often wear jackets and string ties that are color-coordinated with bridesmaids' floor-length gowns. The effect is quite lovely, and is an expression of the wedding party's individuality and down-home style.

It is not at all unusual for mountain men to be buried in a blue-serge shirt, new bib overalls, and a matching overall jacket. Sometimes they requested that attire in advance, or their families knew what they would have preferred. The idea is the man wore comfortable clothes on earth, and he would want to be just as comfortable in his eternal rest.

Grandpa would agree with such practicality and comfort because he wore bib overalls all his life. Mr. Levi Strauss

could not have imagined the future popularity of his original "waist-overalls" sewed from the canvas he had planned
to sell for tents and wagon covers.

Think about old-fashioned photos in family albums that
show men and boys dressed in bib overalls or blue jeans.
Can you recall stories about their preferences for wearing
them for work or as signature styles of clothing? Have you
known older men that you would have difficulty recognizing
if they weren't dressed in overalls or jeans?

73. *Illustrations from a 1923 Sears Catalog feature overalls for men,*
along with "Dad's little helper" sizes.

A good iron wash pot was valued and used for generations

In the antebellum 1800s, plantation owners and other wealthy Southern families brought slaves to cook and wash clothes at their Flat Rock summer homes. Despite losing much of their wealth in the Civil War, they still maintained a sense of gracious living. In 1865, estate owners employed local people for summer positions, and Grandpa's mother, Jane Surrett Russell, was among those hired.

Jane, who was in her early twenties when the war ended, felt fortunate to develop a lifelong career as a laundress. Subsistence farming had generally been the only means of livelihood since settlers came to Western North Carolina. In that agrarian culture, employment opportunities for young ladies simply hadn't existed before the Civil War.

Mountain girls had been taught to wash and iron from an early age, so Jane was already experienced. Excited about her new job, she built fires under the iron pot at the summer residence and efficiently washed clothes and linens for the entire household. Being a diligent and hard worker, she won favor with the mistress of the estate.

Realizing that Jane was to be married soon, the kind lady gave her the iron wash pot at the end of the summer of 1865. Comparable to a washer/drier today, it was a very expensive and useful wedding gift.

74. *The 1865 iron washpot was still in good condition when Janie Mae donated it for posterity to Mountain Heritage Center Museum at Western Carolina University.*

This benevolent lady's name has been lost in history, which is truly regrettable. She was a very caring person who took Jane with her to worship at Saint John in the Wilderness Episcopal Church in Flat Rock.

When Jane began her family, she combined her laundress experience with the gift of the fine wash pot to begin her own business. Rather than working at the summer homes, she now picked up and delivered their laundry. She was a lady entrepreneur before it was fashionable, and her skills supported the family after her husband became crippled.

Energetic and determined (headstrong, actually) Jane washed clothes all day and ironed most of the night. To keep up with the demands of her business, she regularly went to bed at 4:00 a.m. when other farm families were rising.

Decades later, Granny told the story of the neighbors not understanding Jane's work schedule and watching for mid-morning smoke in her chimney. They had chores done and half the garden hoed by the time Jane got up, so they disparagingly said, "She must be awful lazy!"

Granny always defended her mother-in-law and empathized with the burdens of her life. Jane took pride in her work, and she was careful to take very good care of the wedding-gift wash pot until she finally had to retire—after fifty years.

Though there were closer relatives, Jane chose to give the wash pot to Granny. In appreciation of her mother-in-law's gift, Granny carefully used it—for forty more years—before placing it in storage. Decades later, I was honored to inherit the 1865 wedding present.

In memory of the kindness of the Flat Rock estate lady, and the hard work of both Great-Grandma Jane and Granny, I donated the valued iron wash pot to Mountain Heritage Center Museum at Western Carolina University.

The curator was amazed at its good condition. The iron legs were still intact, and it was not burned or rusted. Each generation had taken very good care of the wonderful wedding gift from 1865.

Can you recall stories about antiques that were passed down through the generations in your family? Especially think of those that might have been used in their working years.

Clothes were boiled in an iron wash pot

Today, laundry can be done anytime we toss a load into the washer/drier. In an hour, we can hang the clothes in the closet since modern fabrics require very little ironing. Wash day was vastly different years ago. As the sun peeked around Hogback Mountain, Granny gathered clothes and tied them in a sheet. Lifting the bundle onto her back, she carried it down the trail to the wash place which was a level area below the spring.

There, the iron wash pot (from 1865) was set on rocks to allow space for fire, and spring water flowed through a spout and splashed into a galvanized tub.

The wash place was a pleasant spot for me to play when I was four, going on five. Pretty moss grew along the bank, and I enjoyed the murmur of running water. It gurgled down the rocky stream as I dabbled in the washtub under the spout.

Wash day wasn't a play day for Granny, though.

The first task was to fill the wash pot ¾ full of water and add chips of homemade lye soap. Then she built a quick hot fire, gradually piling on heavier wood. I "helped" by adding twigs to the blaze. A curl of faint, blue smoke spiraled toward the treetops as flames leaped under the wash pot.

She dipped white clothes in the near-boiling water. This was the first step for their being "battled" on the battling block with the battling stick.

The battling block was a split log (set on posts). Granny used the hickory battling stick Grandpa had whittled to resemble a short, wide boat paddle. Lathering each wet garment and placing it on the block, she began to beat it with the battling stick—like it was a snake "fixin" to bite her!

Playing at the water spout, I listened to the "whomp, whomp" sounds echoing through the woods as Granny worked up a sweat wielding the heavy stick. If that effort didn't remove a stain, she grabbed a rippled-metal scrub board and rubbed it out.

When Granny was satisfied the garment was clean, she scooped it off the battling block into the now-boiling wash pot. Soap bubbled and popped as she stirred with the battling stick.

Every now and again, she'd stop and add wood to keep the water boiling. Clouds of hickory smoke swirled as she tended the fire all morning. After a time of boiling and stirring, with smoke blowing in her eyes, she transferred the wet clothes to the tub under the spout. When the white things were rinsed and wrung out, the same battling-boiling process began with the dark clothes.

Modern garments wouldn't last through one washing.

The fabrics in those days were tougher.

The people were, too.

By midday, Granny dumped buckets of water onto the fire and emptied the laundry water which helped put the coals completely out. Then, she tipped the iron wash pot upside down to prevent rust.

Finally, it was time to pack the wet laundry into buckets for the first of several trips up the spring trail to the clothesline in the yard. She was always proud of the dazzling whiteness of her sheets; They did look pretty fluttering in mountain breezes beside the brilliant flowers.

In later years, Granny often declared, "Washing machines just don't clean my clothes as good as the old iron wash pot and battlin' block." Her work ethic was so strong the word "automatic" never became a part of her vocabulary.

Recall how laundry was done in your grandmothers' day, and compare the time and effort with modern methods.

Clotheslines, sadirons, and homemade starch were common

In Granny's lifetime, clothes were boiled in iron wash pots over hickory fires, rinsed under waterspouts in galvanized tubs, and hung on clotheslines. Laundry required an entire morning, though she started at sunrise. When the clothes were finally boiled and rinsed at the wash place, she carried them up the steep trail to the clothesline in the yard.

Her washday preference was a breezy, sunny day so the laundry would dry by late afternoon. It helped if just the sheets and thinner garments dried the first day they were hung on the clothesline.

The option of leaving heavier clothes out overnight or bringing them inside to be rehung the next day was not appealing, though Granny made that choice many times over the years.

Back then, the weekly process of washing, drying, starching, and ironing required three days, even in good weather.

The second day was used to starch shirts, dresses, aprons, and ruffled, flour-sack curtains. However, starch didn't come in spray cans back then. Granny cooked it on the woodstove using the traditional recipe: One cup of flour and one cup of sugar carefully mixed with four cups of water.

She stirred this gluey concoction constantly until it boiled and thickened (about 25-30 minutes). Homemade starch turned shiny like pudding when it was properly cooked. Gradually, Granny thinned it with cold water to produce the stiffness required for a particular garment. Then she dipped each piece several times and hung it on the clothesline—to dry again.

On the third day, these stiff-as-a-board garments were dampened and ironed with the rest of the freshly washed clothing. Granny heated three sadirons on the wood cookstove and rotated them so she could always have a hot iron ready. An all-day fire in the kitchen felt good in winter, but it was almost unbearable in summertime.

75. One of Granny's sadirons remained, and Janie Mae donated it
for posterity to Mountain Heritage Center Museum,
Western Carolina University.

Using a pot holder, she removed a hot iron from the stove and quickly rubbed it over a piece of beeswax. This helped the iron not to stick, because the flour-based starch in the clothes scorched quite easily.

Grandpa wanted his dress clothing, bib overalls, and work shirts carefully pressed with distinct creases in the pants and sleeves. Even red-bandana handkerchiefs had to be ironed and folded in neat squares to fit in his back pocket, so Granny spent quite a long time ironing each piece to perfection. Her starched aprons, cotton dresses, and ruffled, flour-sack curtains required careful attention, too.

Throughout the day she kept the fire stoked and continued to rotate each cooling iron for yet another hot one from the stove. Finally, the week's laundry was done; The freshly ironed kitchen curtains were returned to the windows, and clothes were hung in the mirrored chifforobe or folded in bureau drawers.

Washing, starching, and ironing was indeed a three-day process on Bear Mountain. Of course, Granny could have completed the task more quickly by eliminating the homemade starch and not ironing some garments.

However, she always said she didn't want Grandpa to look all "wrinkledy" and "half-seen about" like he was "batching." That was the term mountain folks used to describe a situation where a man lived alone (like a bachelor) and didn't have a wife to take care of him. Granny took quite a bit of pride in stirring up a pan of starch and ironing Grandpa's clothes to perfection.

Think about the way ironing was done at an older relative's home years ago.

Can you recall memories of starched clothes you may have worn as a child?

Mountain folks carried water from the spring

Spring water continues to be popular in the 21st century, but not in the same way it was a hundred years ago. Now, we buy individual bottles of pure spring water—to carry along on our exercise walks.

Times have changed.

In the old days, mountain folks exercised by walking to the spring—and carrying buckets of pure spring water for the entire household.

When Granny and Grandpa bought their scenic home place in 1917 (and again in 1927) a major selling point was the fresh-water spring. Because the high mineral content of the area often caused a metallic flavor, such sweet-tasting water was highly valued.

On their mountain, an abundant supply of good water bubbled from the ground and filled a sandy basin at the bottom of the steepest ridge. Since the 1800s, hefty rocks had kept the dirt sidewalls intact, and water from this deep, natural spring was icy cold, even in summer.

It would seem like a problem to us that the water was at the bottom of the hill, and the house was at the top of the hill. However, in those days, country folks expected the spring to be down the mountain from the house.

76. *The 1895 spring on Bear Mountain still flows in the 21ˢᵗ century.*

It would be decades before most rural homes in the South enjoyed the luxury of running water, particularly before the era of FDR and the TVA. Therefore, carrying water on a mountain farm in the 1920s seemed to be as normal as the sunrise. In my grandparents' opinion, it was easy to grab a couple of buckets, hike down the trail, dip the cold, fresh water, and carry it back to the house.

They had running water—all they had to do was run and get it.

It is interesting to realize that water weighs over eight pounds per gallon, and that the average farm bucket held three gallons. Carrying two buckets at a time up the spring trail would be a tough job for most of us.

Imagine the number of daily trips required for family cooking, drinking, dishwashing, bathing and housecleaning. Then, consider the seasonal duties of sterilizing several hundred glass jars to pickle, preserve, and can the summer fruit and vegetable harvest.

Granny was known to cook big company meals, and she was a tidy housekeeper. Considering the energy required to carry it up the steep hill, she never seemed to be sparing in the use of water.

Because of the remote location, electricity would not become available in their section of Henderson County until 1975. So, during their years on the beloved mountain, they continued to carry water—two buckets at a time.

Like other practical people of their era, Granny and Grandpa simply adjusted to living on a rural farm. Instead of complaining, they celebrated the many benefits, one of which was good water. Over the years, they became quite partial to their own spring. They barely tolerated well water and certainly disliked city water (the few times they tasted it).

Although they appreciated natural spring water, my grandparents would have difficulty believing it is sold nowadays in 16.9-ounce bottles—and is used for hydration on exercise walks.

Like other "lily-livered" modern folks, I certainly don't exercise by carrying water buckets; it's easier to turn on the faucet. Imagine what Granny would think of my pushbutton dishwashing—especially when plenty of water still flows in her old-timey spring (a mere quarter mile down the hill).

Can you recall a particularly cold and good spring, perhaps at an ancestor's home place?

If a bucket had a hole in it, Granny still found it useful

Granny had probably heard the witty country song about a make-believe bucket with a hole in it. But Granny didn't throw real buckets away—even after they were worn out and really did have holes in them. To her way of thinking, they could still be used for something.

Leather or wooden buckets were common before rust-proof, galvanized buckets were manufactured in the 1800s. Time seemed to move slowly on Bear Mountain, so metal buckets, in whatever condition, were still necessary in the 1900s.

Granny's water and feed buckets had been bought new at Walker's Hardware on Hendersonville's King Street. Others, including lard buckets, were simply kept and reused.

Granny preferred homemade lard, rendered at hog-killing time, as long as it lasted. Then, Grandpa bought four-pound metal pails of pure lard at Maybin's Grocery in Zirconia, or sometimes at Hill's Grocery in East Flat Rock. Those small buckets were saved because they had tight-fitting lids and were perfect for storing nails, jar lids or other little objects.

Lard buckets had wire handles, too, and were often used as school-lunch pails. They would also be carried on day trips across the mountains to pick blackberries and huckle-berries. After picnicking and filling the larger berry pails, a few extra berries could be taken home in the now-empty lunch buckets.

77. Leon Morgan displays buckets of many sizes available at the M.A. Pace General Store in Saluda, NC.

Syrup and molasses pails were smaller, but also had wire handles and nice lids. To promote brand names, syrup producers often used clever advertising. One company famously declared their syrup was so tasty it gave a biscuit a "college education."

And on winter mornings, country folks certainly agreed. They still remember hot biscuits—straight from the woodstove—split, buttered and slathered with thick syrup.

Emptied pails were convenient for storing buttons, thread, marbles, coins or balls of string. In the kitchen, a designated bacon-grease bucket was handy to dip into when making gravy or seasoning beans.

Farmhouses in Granny's era didn't feature built-in cabinets with shelves and drawers that are standard in modern homes. So, it was not unusual to see an assortment of metal buckets hanging from the ceilings, rafters, or walls of country homes and barns. They were filled with a variety of things-to-keep—or simply saved as empty containers that were ready to be used in a jiffy.

Humidity in old-fashioned houses was a problem, too. Matches, a valuable item, were often stored in repurposed pails with lids that helped to control humidity. Soggy, damp matches wouldn't strike, so it was important to keep them dry to be able to kindle the cooking fires that were made daily.

Plastic pails wouldn't be invented until 1967, so products needing sturdy containers were always packaged in metal when Granny and Grandpa lived on the mountain.

Larger, galvanized pails from the hardware store were useful as feed buckets for cows, pigs and chickens. These were generally shallower than water buckets and were quite a bit wider.

Extras were handy for gathering tomatoes, cucumbers and squash from the garden. Potatoes or apples could be toted from the can-house storage bins when Granny needed more than she could carry in her upturned apron. She thought it took a bucketful of potatoes to cook one of her company dinners.

On wash day, she took laundry down the mountain, boiled clothes in the iron wash pot, and rinsed them under the water spout. Then she packed the heavy, wet garments in galvanized buckets and carried them uphill to the clothesline in the yard.

Milk pails were smaller than water buckets but were perfect for use in the barn. Granny sat on the three-legged stool and squirted cow milk into those buckets every day for decades. Typically, the capacity of metal water buckets was between two and three gallons (weighing over 20 pounds when filled). Several times a day, Granny carried two buckets at a time up the spring trail. Preparing meals from scratch, dishwashing, bathing and housecleaning (to Granny's standards) required a lot of water.

It may be surprising to us modern folks, but a worn-out bucket with a hole in it really was useful on the farm. Granny liked to have several on hand for growing special flowers. The more the buckets leaked, the better the drainage was for a potted plant, in her opinion. She displayed such discards beside the steps and would enjoy the blooms all summer.

There was a story about country children coming upon a large snake near their spring. Dropping their water buckets, they ran screaming to the house. Their courageous mother brought a gun, but a bullet ricocheted off creek rocks and hit one of the buckets.

In all the commotion, the snake slithered away. But after that scary episode, the kids enjoyed carrying water in the bucket with a hole in it. Since it only held half as much, the bullet-riddled pail wasn't nearly so heavy. (The poisonous snake was later found and chopped into small pieces with a shovel. And they made a special trip to Walker's Hardware for a new bucket.)

Another use for leaky buckets was to place them upside down on support posts when constructing a corncrib. Granny explained that field mice were able to climb six feet off the ground into the log building and eat the corn, but the destructive little critters couldn't get past the slippery metal buckets on top of the posts.

Country folks never minded that each support pillar seemed to display a different kind of worn-out bucket. I remember some castoffs still being shiny enough to reflect the morning sun—from their last assignment underneath the tall corncrib. And I thought Granny was smart to protect the winter corn with buckets that had holes in them.

But I never did figure out why Granny and Grandpa built the hog pen so far up the mountain from the water source. As a child I saw pigs in it, and the hand-dug depression of that pen is still recognizable in the hillside (over seven decades later).

Considering that one hog requires up to five gallons of water daily, the thought of carrying so many heavy buckets—up the steep hill, through the cornfield, across the yard, and out the stagecoach trail was formidable. Maintaining sufficient hydration for growing piglets, especially in hot summer months, required multiple pails of fresh water brought to the pen seven days a week.

An easier alternative would have been to build the pen closer to the creek. Since water was already piped from the spring, bucketsful could easily have been dumped into the pigs' water troughs. It seems to me that keeping the thirsty creatures even a quarter-of-a-mile closer would have been more convenient.

In retrospect, I realize that my grandparents probably were concerned that the entire tributary would become contaminated despite their best efforts. So, they carried hundreds of buckets of water up the mountain to the pigpen.

Traditionally, Granny and Grandpa's generation was thoughtful and considerate of other people—including unknown neighbors who lived miles downstream.

Similar stories may have been passed down in your family, along with memories of galvanized water and feed buckets. Can you imagine ways that farm folks might have used a bucket with a hole in it?

Ask the oldest person you know if she or he remembers when syrup, molasses and lard came in metal pails with handles and lids. What treasures or necessities were stored in the repurposed buckets?

Are you familiar with the mountain expression, "... couldn't carry a tune in a bucket?" In the era when country folks were familiar with carrying water in buckets, the adage was used as self-deprecating humor: "You know I can't sing; I couldn't carry a tune in a bucket." (Maybe their imaginary bucket had a hole in it.)

The Sears-Roebuck catalog was a window to the world

I n our "Information Age" it might be difficult to comprehend the significance of Sears, Roebuck & Co. in the lives
of several generations of mountain people. Comparable to
the World-Wide Web, the company's picture catalog was a
window to the outside world. Necessities, unfamiliar luxuries, boots, hammers, Sunday hats, coffeepots, harmonicas,
mantle clocks, or even live, baby chickens could be selected
from over a thousand pages.

And in just a few days, such diverse items could be delivered in rural Appalachia by Parcel Post. The Sears-Roebuck
catalog was truly the old-time equivalent of Amazon.com
for our great-grandparents. Country folks born during the
first half of the twentieth century grew up with the thick,
picture book in their homes.

My earliest catalog memories, at age three, illustrate the
extent of that societal and generational influence. Living
several miles from town, I was already familiar with placing catalog orders. When my new shoes were ordered, I
"helped" look at catalog pictures, and the shoes arrived in
the mailbox.

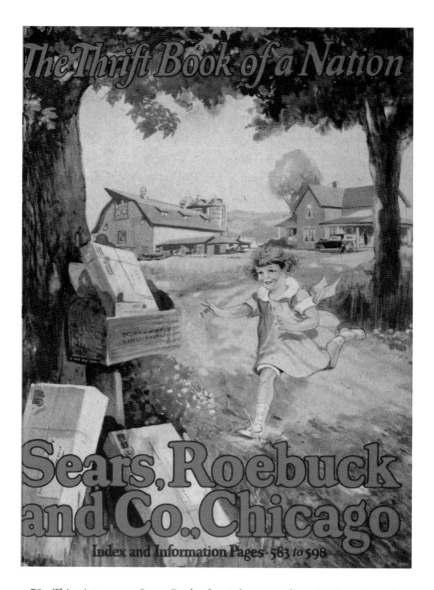

78. This picturesque Sears-Roebuck catalog cover from 1922 captures the excitement of rural families. In 1913, the Post Office began delivering packages along with the mail. The new concept became very popular, particularly in rural areas, and the number of Sears-catalog recipients soon doubled. This 1922 edition went to 4,393,746 homes—approximately one catalog for every 6 homes in the United States.

So, when my parents announced I would soon have a baby brother, I immediately placed the Sears-Roebuck catalog onto the floor and turned to the baby-clothes section. Looking through the pictures, I chose the prettiest one—and I was assured that exact baby would arrive via Parcel Post.

Somehow, I wasn't confused when Baby Brother actually came home in an ambulance driven by "Santa Claus." But the initial concept of my earliest-childhood thinking was that everything I received came from Sears-Roebuck. Apparently, I learned early because mountain folks like my family had already depended on the catalog for three generations.

Published in 1888, Richard W. Sears' first edition featured watches and jewelry. But by 1893, he partnered with A. C. Roebuck to expand the business. The Sears, Roebuck & Co. catalogs soon displayed thousands of items over hundreds of pages.

The continuing development of Rural Free Delivery by the early 1900s meant that more farm folks could receive a catalog in their new mailboxes. In 1913, the Post Office added Parcel Post package delivery to rural routes. Now, the outside world came by the boxful to the "doorsteps" of farm families.

Country people, who seldom left farm chores to shop in distant towns, could have goods delivered by the mailman. From the convenience of the kitchen table, farmers could make selections and complete order forms for things they needed.

In poorer homes, the Sears-Roebuck catalog was sometimes the only book besides the Bible, and it was displayed just as prominently. Placing a minimum order kept a family on the company's mailing list for the next issue. So, a current catalog became a status symbol as well as a readily available source of knowledge about the outside world.

Before television, looking at the so-called "Sears Wish Book" provided hours of informative entertainment. Even when they couldn't afford to shop, country people learned about new styles and trends. Farmers wanted to know about steel traps and the newest plow attachments. Ladies were curious about the width of hat brims for spring. Fashionable skirts might be straighter, fuller, longer, or shorter during the coming season, and country women used that information when sewing their own clothes.

Like other talented farmwives, Granny referred to the Sears-Roebuck catalog for fashion guidance. A family story from the 1920s recalls that Granny sewed up-to-date school clothes for her daughter. Even without paper patterns, she copied the little-girls' styles shown in the catalog. Although Granny used fabrics she had on hand, the dresses, skirts, and matching jackets incorporated the latest fashion trends of that era. And the stylish outfits were highly complimented by other children.

Over the years, mountain people like Granny and Grandpa ordered new shoes and necessities as they could afford them. As times got better, Granny enjoyed choosing decorations for the house. I remember her attractive living-room window shades and sheer, ruffled, Pricilla-style curtains. The dark-green shades were fringed at the bottom and featured tasseled pull-cords. When they were raised, the thin curtains let in a maximum amount of light. Granny liked that combination; she would have felt insecure with see-through curtains without window shades.

She had "studied" the catalog for an hour or two before choosing those styles. (Her quaint, descriptive verb showed the level of concentration necessary to make such important decisions.) She still sewed ruffled, flour-sack curtains for the kitchen. But the "front room" was special, and she wanted it to look modern—like the pictures she saw in the catalog.

Another decorative, household purchase was a new linoleum rug, carefully chosen from Sears-Roebuck. Large roses with green, trailing vines shown on burgundy backgrounds were popular then, and Granny kept a fairly new linoleum in each room.

However, bringing the long, rolled-up package to the mountain required two people. Even Parcel Post couldn't deliver where there were no roads. Granny and Grandpa had to walk two miles to the Zirconia Post Office and carry the new rug home. But Granny tolerated occasional inconvenience to make the house look nice.

Perhaps the most unusual item Granny ordered from Sears-Roebuck was a dry sink. Even without running water, she thought a sink would be convenient for the disposal of dishwater, cooking, and bath water. Instead of carrying heavy pans outside in bad weather, she could simply pour used water down the drain.

After "studying" catalog pictures, she realized she could make her plan work. Being talented at rough carpentry, Granny built a kitchen cabinet with a proper-sized opening for the new sink. She figured ways to install a drain pipe through the floor, underneath the house, and down the hill where she'd been tossing water, anyway.

Then she placed the order to Sears-Roebuck. But all necessary piping wasn't included when the sink arrived, so she had to place a second order. Still, she considered her idea to be brilliant and wondered how she managed all those years without her new, dry sink.

The catalog illustrations enabled Granny to visualize contemporary options that could be adapted to her country lifestyle, and she appreciated any convenience on Bear Mountain. Once again, the Sears-Roebuck catalog provided a window to the outside world for farm folks.

During my childhood, well-dressed ladies wore hats, and Granny was particularly fond of them because her hair wasn't as thick as it used to be. When ordering a new hat, Granny "studied" the catalog choices.

As she and I turned the pages in the millinery section, Granny pointed out hats worn by older models. When she saw a lady who looked like her, she ordered that hat, even if it was one of the more expensive. Granny felt confident wearing that style, and she was always glad the catalog showed photos and drawings of older women modeling hats and dresses. Sears-Roebuck certainly understood their traditional, rural customer base.

Although Granny continued to sew everyday cotton dresses, she ordered a few Sunday clothes. By "studying" styles, fabrics, and colors, she chose classic designs that looked fashionable for several years. I especially remember her soft, blue dress for special occasions. In the catalog it may have been "worn" by a lady who looked a lot like Granny.

Perhaps some of your older friends remember depictions of more-matronly models. Think of your early memories of Sears-Roebuck, as well. Try to recall special or unusual items your family ordered—back when the picture catalog was indeed a window to the world.

Leather shoes were valued and repaired in Grandpa's time

Today leather shoes are taken for granted. Few people remember going barefoot in summer, much less during winter. But there are true stories about mountain children tying sacks around their feet to walk to school in the snow. No wonder leather shoes were valued.

In Grandpa's day "shoe leather was downright skeerce" as he expressed it. Therefore, when folks could get shoes, they needed to be worn as long as possible. I remember new soles and heels being nailed onto "perfectly good shoes that just need a little mending." Since it was cheaper to buy new heels and soles and attach them at home, Grandpa kept the old-fashioned "shoe last" for that purpose.

In fact, that cast-iron cobblers' shoe implement was considered to be an antique only when I inherited it. During Grandpa's lifetime it was a necessary household item. Living on the secluded mountain, my grandparents walked two miles to the grocery store and Post Office. On the farm, they walked by necessity to carry water, cut wood, and grow gardens. Their shoes received a lot of wear, especially during Grandpa's working years.

Back when Grandpa was a young man, new work boots cost approximately $2.00. That was a lot considering that the "best job in the country" paid ten cents per hour. Fortunately, he was hired at Southern Railway where the hours were long, and the pay was good.

But even after retirement, he continued nailing on new heels and half soles. He and Granny never forgot the value of leather shoes.

79. *Grandpa regularly used this cast-iron, repair implement to attach new heels and half-soles to "perfectly good shoes that just need a little mending." It is now displayed at Mountain Heritage Center Museum on the campus of Western Carolina University.*

Packages of shoe tacks, replacement heels, and soles were available at F.W. Woolworth's 5 and 10 Cent Store on Hendersonville's Main Street, and Grandpa liked to keep supplies on hand. As I watched, he would ceremoniously turn the worn shoe upside down on the shoe iron. Using a hammer, he would lightly pound little tacks into new heels and soles and proudly announce, "Now, these shoes will last another year or two."

It was difficult for Grandpa to comprehend why good shoes were no longer passed down from older girls to younger boys. Folks tried to explain that in the 1950s, little boys couldn't wear their sisters' outgrown socks to school— and certainly not girls' shoes. Grandpa just shook his head and wondered what the world was coming to; he reckoned that "times shore had changed" since he was young.

"People's gettin' to be plum wasteful," he figured, and Granny recalled a story that further supported such old-time values. Also using Appalachian English, she explained, "Back in the early 1900s, mountain boys had to be real practical and notice a girl's thrifty ways when they's lookin' for a wife.

"When I was coming up," she told me, "leather shoes was so costly folks only wore'em on Sunday, and then only when they's in sight of the church." She remembered when mountain people, including young ladies, walked barefoot from home to "save shoe leather."

As I listened in total fascination, Granny continued, "Back then, they carried the fine shoes in their arms to the last ridge at Crossroads Baptist Church in Zirconia. Thrifty girls set down under the big oak tree to put on their shoes. And after church, they stopped there again to take the shoes off a'fore walkin' home.

"The local boys in the group just stood off and sorta watched which girls walked the dusty road wearin' expensive shoes—and which ones waited to put'em on when they's in sight of the church. They knowed if a young lady was so thoughtless about the cost of shoe leather, she'd be a pore manager of a farmhouse."

Granny further explained, "A boy wouldn't ever set his cap for a girl like that. He thought she'd prob'ly throw more out the back door than he could bring in the front door."

Although I couldn't relate to those levels of thrift, it is remarkable that I was privileged to hear such direct, oral history from so long ago. Granny's story was not legend or folklore, but a first-person description of life in Henderson County at the turn of the 20th century. As she finished telling about the old days, Granny always said she "shore was glad that times had changed."

During my childhood, Granny and Grandpa had "everyday" shoes, as well as dress shoes that they wore to funerals and for special occasions. I always admired Grandpa's shiny, patent-leather Sunday shoes. In retrospect, I realize just how special they must have been to him.

Every time the expensive shoes were worn, he shined them with a biscuit that had been left over from breakfast. Grandpa explained that the pure lard Granny mixed into the biscuits was just oily enough to remove dirt and dust. Polishing with a soft, crumbly biscuit made patent-leather look brand-new again. After being thoroughly cleaned, Sunday shoes were prudently stored in the bottom of the chifforobe.

Cared for with liquid polish, Granny's dress shoes looked remarkably similar to her everyday shoes. Sunday shoes were newer, but the styles were the same. Granny liked lace-up shoes with wide heels almost 2 inches tall since she said, "The height makes my back feel better." Such "clunky" heels were going out of fashion, and slim heels were coming in. But Granny preferred comfort and practicality over style.

It was amusing to watch my aged Granny, wearing those cumbersome, high-heeled shoes, when she was chasing a chicken through the yard. If she took a notion for chicken and dumplings, Granny could run quite well—and flap her apron at the same time. She always cornered the squawking chicken, too! As a small child, I thought such skirmishes were exciting and entertaining on the normally quiet mountain.

Typically, Granny and Grandpa ordered new shoes from the Sears-Roebuck catalog. It showed pages of current and traditional styles for men and women. The company understood their customer base and always included designs country people had become accustomed to over the years.

But during World War II, purchasing new shoes was challenging because soldiers' needs were prioritized. Those years of rationing must have reminded my grandparents of their youth when "shoe leather was hard to come by." A full page of special-ordering instructions was included in wartime editions of Sears-Roebuck catalogs, along with helpful information.

80. *During World War II, Sears-Roebuck catalogs included special instructions for ordering rationed shoes. Even the government considered shoe leather "hard to come by." Granny and Grandpa understood because they had valued leather shoes all their lives. This copy is from Janie Mae's collection of vintage catalogs.*

If a family had used their allotment of Ration Stamps, they could apply at the local Rationing Board for exemptions based on need. Employees who provided essential services (nurses, mailmen, factory, and farm workers) could request permission to purchase extra shoes.

However, the instructions indicated that rubber boots for work required a special certificate—separate from Ration Stamp No. 1, or Ration Stamp No. 2, from Ration Book No. 3. Such detailed regulations must have been confusing to Granny and Grandpa, but they were willing to comply to help win the war. In those days, even the government considered shoe leather "hard to come by." And my grandparents understood—because they had always lived that way.

Ask the oldest people you know about new shoes being rationed in wartime; they will have first-person accounts that are worthy of being passed down. They may recall barefoot children in summer and times when leather shoes were highly valued and repaired at home. And a few older folks may remember shining patent-leather shoes with biscuits.

Concepts of feminine beauty changed over the years

When Granny was a teenager in the early 1900s, opinions of feminine beauty were quite different than they were in the prosperous post-war years. She just couldn't understand the teen fads of my 1950s age group.

The popular trend of girls lying in the sun to get tans seemed especially incomprehensible.

"Back in my day," Granny often explained, "young ladies wore long dresses and big bonnets, anyway. Then, to hoe corn in the sunshine, we pulled thick, cotton stockings over our hands and arms. Such an outfit was awful hot, but we wanted to keep our skin looking good."

Isn't it remarkable that in the 21st century, medical professionals have proved Granny's old-fashioned beauty idea to be correct? Now, young and old alike are encouraged to wear floppy hats and long sleeves in the sun. Entire new industries have developed to manufacture sunscreen products for children and adults.

*81. Longer, flowing dresses like these were stylish
when Granny was a young woman.*

Granny was also quite puzzled by teen girls of my era who
dieted to look slim and trim. "Times have changed," she

reckoned. "In the old days, a mountain feller wouldn't even think of courtin' a scrawny girl.

"He figured such a woman would always be sickly and cost him lots of doctor bills. She wouldn't be able to hoe the garden—much less plow the cornfields. She'd be too frail and spindling to chop wood, and probably couldn't carry a bucket of water from the spring."

Granny described the ideal physique in the early 1900s: "A mountain boy wanted a stout girl, a little on the chunky side. He reckoned she'd be better suited to work on his farm, and to raise him a family of little farmhands."

Granny used the word "chunky" but she probably hadn't heard the legend of Chunky Gal Mountain. The tall peak towers 4,400 feet in North Carolina's Clay County (near the Tennessee border).

In folklore, the mountain was named for an above-average-sized Indian princess. She stubbornly refused to marry the young warrior chosen by her father, the chief.

Instead, the hefty maiden ran away to wed a lover from another tribe. The last place she was seen became known as Chunky Gal Mountain. It retains that name to this day and has become a popular backpacking destination for tourists.

Times do change, and concepts of feminine beauty change with them. Mountain fellows no longer choose a wife based on her ability to plow cornfields (thank goodness). Granny couldn't identify with modern ideas of dieting, because in her day grueling farm work might have been too much for a frail girl.

It is interesting that 21st-century modeling agencies have been disciplined for allowing young ladies to diet too strenuously. Doctors know that the desire to be thin can lead to anorexia and bulimia. These disorders cause long-term health problems that were unknown in previous generations when fuller figures were preferred.

"Normal" weight may differ from one era to another, but I like to think a "chunky" girl is prettier and healthier, too.

Modern doctors now agree that Granny's old-fashioned idea of protecting the skin from harmful sunrays is medically correct.

Her view of dieting is probably right, as well.

It might be interesting to recall stories about perceptions of beauty when your grandmother was a teenager. Think of fads from your younger days that she (or older relatives) couldn't understand.

Harmonicas were popular musical instruments in the mountains

H armonicas were commonly called "French harps" or "mouth organs," and mountain men played them superbly. Some still do, though such old-fashioned music is not nearly as common as it was before and during the Great Depression. Back then, hearing a live imitation of a steam train (complete with the wailing whistle) was marvelous entertainment on Saturday nights. The small instrument had the capability of alternately rumbling, wheezing, chugging—and whistling—like a real train climbing a steep, Appalachian mountain.

Almost any country song, ballad, or hymn could be performed by talented country folks on the inexpensive, portable harmonica. A man was never truly alone, even in a remote mountain cabin, with a "French harp" in his pocket. Early Sears-Roebuck catalogs listed harmonicas for as little as 27 cents, though their most popular Hohner cost 58 cents. Even that was not an insurmountable amount of money for so much entertainment.

That's what Mr. Matthias Hohner had in mind when he developed the first Hohner harmonica in Germany in 1857.

Since he had relatives who had emigrated to the U.S., he sent them samples for distribution. The simple instrument quickly became popular, and Abraham Lincoln enjoyed carrying a harmonica in his pocket.

During the 1860 presidential debates, Lincoln's exuberant opponent, Stephen Douglas, arrived to the fanfare of his own brass band. Lincoln, however, only had his trusty harmonica. He is credited with saying, "Mr. Douglas needs a brass band, but the harmonica will do for me."

During the Civil War, the Hohner relatives generously shared with soldiers, and such transportable music in lonely camps was appreciated. Later, there was a story about the infamous outlaws, Jesse James and his brother, Frank. Evidently Frank enjoyed playing harmonica music, and according to legend, the little instrument in his pocket once deflected a bullet.

In the late 1800s, an exploration party in the Amazon rainforest was accosted by spear-waving natives. Thinking quickly, one of the team members began playing music on his take-along harmonica. Fascinated, the warriors decided to welcome the foreigners and listen to more music. In another instance, aboriginals were given peace-offering gifts of shiny harmonicas. But their skimpy jungle attire had no pockets in which to carry them. So, they resolved the problem by happily attaching their new harmonicas to necklaces—which was handier, anyway.

In the following decades, "French harps" were sold by the hundreds of thousands around the world and across the United States. The small instrument became commonplace in Appalachian mountain homes, and special brands were often passed down through the generations.

When radio and 78-rpm records became available in the 20th century, folks could appreciate the talents of more-professional harmonica players. They never tired of hearing the

Orange Blossom Special, a popular harmonica tune about a fast-moving train. Since he had been a railroad man for over forty years, Grandpa especially enjoyed listening to train songs on his battery radio.

Out west, the lonesome cowboys carried harmonicas in their saddlebags and played *Home on the Range* around campfires: *Oh, give me a home where the buffalo roam... and the skies are not cloudy all day....* The melancholy, lingering sounds were said to calm the cows as they rested on their long journey. Some pocket-harp enthusiasts still insist that slow songs are the most beautiful. A real treat, then and now, is the haunting tune of *Red River Valley* on harmonica: *"...Come and sit by my side if you love me. Do not hasten to bid me adieu. But remember the Red River Valley, and the one who has loved you so true...."*

As a child, I enjoyed hearing *The Wayfaring Stranger* expertly played in a country church. Written in a mournful, minor key, the song was perfect for the slow-harmonica performance: *I am a poor wayfaring stranger a-traveling through this world below. But there's no sickness, toil, or danger in that bright land to which I go....*

Older gentlemen still play harmonicas in the few mountain churches that continue to include country and bluegrass musical instruments. At Scenic Hills Baptist Church, Mr. Oscar Anderson regularly performs *If I Could Hear My Mother Pray Again,* alternating between the harmonica and singing the poignant words. With guitar and bass fiddle accompaniment, his harmonica carries the tearful, wavering-tenor melody of childhood memories: *How sweet and happy seem those days of which I dream...if I could hear my mother pray again....*

82. Oscar Anderson plays harmonica back-up for Bill Gordon, guitarist/soloist with the Royal Blue Gospel Bluegrass Band: (left to right) Norman Whitfield, guitar; Duane Ragan, lap steel guitar; Joanie Sanders, guitar; Bob Dockery, bass fiddle; Bill Gordon; Oscar Anderson; Lewis Pace, banjo.

Like many farm boys in the South, Mr. Oscar picked cotton every summer. With those earnings, he ordered one of his first harmonicas from Wayne Raney and Lonnie Glosson's nationwide radio broadcast. Playing music on 200 radio stations, they reportedly sold 5 million "talking harmonicas" by mail order. During folksy radio shows, they advertised the lowly pocket harp (with a free instruction booklet) as an affordable alternative to more-expensive musical instruments.

Raney and Glosson's combined musical talent and down-home salesmanship made $2.00 harmonicas very attractive to country folks. After all, Wayne Raney had been performing since age eleven, and Lonnie had been almost that young when he began playing the harmonica on street corners. Rural radio listeners could appreciate such hard-scrabble determination and musical talent. And like young Oscar Anderson, they wanted to learn to play the harmonica, too.

83. Employee Johnnie Blackwell plays harmonica at Tempo Music Center. Michael Hall, seated at right, owner of the Hendersonville music store, sells 15-20 harmonicas every month. The Hohner, first manufactured in Germany in 1858, remains popular in the mountains today.

Even in modern times, Mr. Hohner's original idea of selling a small, playable musical instrument at a low price holds true. On Hendersonville's Main Street, Tempo Music Center continues to carry the mountain tradition of harmonica music into the 21st century. They regularly sell 15 to 20 "French harps" nearly every month. "Student" harmonicas can be purchased for $15.00 or less, though professional models are about $200.00.

Local musicians appreciate being able to shop on Historic Main Street for traditional-sounding harmonicas, complete with the latest accessories. Old-time harmonicists who also played guitar always needed to use their hands to strum chords while continuing to play the harmonica. Creatively, they bent wire coat hangers around their necks and inserted the harmonica in front. The handy (but uncomfortable) idea

caught on, and companies began manufacturing professional harmonica holders. Often constructed to fit a particular brand, they are usually in stock at Tempo, and high-end
designs are close to a hundred dollars. That is more than a
sack full of harmonicas used to cost, but bluegrass musicians
enjoy the convenience and comfort of the improved version.

Would you believe that pulmonary rehabilitation classes
highly recommend harmonica playing as a part of medical treatment? Necessary breathing exercises for some lung
conditions are similar to those used in harmonica music.
Mountain men never knew they were strengthening their
lungs as they played their favorite train sounds. Doctors
have found that formerly weak participants show marked
improvement in relatively short periods of time without dull,
repetitious breathing exercises. Group respiratory classes
encourage patients to learn together and have fun playing
simple songs.

And the clear, wailing sound of harmonica music is just
as unmistakable now as it was in 1857 when the Hohner
Company began manufacturing them in Germany.

Think about older folks you may have known who played
harmonicas. Would you have preferred the bluegrass-train
sounds, fast songs, or the slow, mournful tunes popular in
the mountains years ago? Consider the rarity of hearing
such an old-fashioned instrument in our modern times.

Little girls played with corncob dolls

O n the mountain farm, corn was gathered and stored in the corncrib to be shelled for the chickens during the winter. When the fall crops were finally harvested, dried, pickled, and canned, Granny had more time to sew than she'd enjoyed in several months. In addition to making curtains, aprons, and everyday dresses for herself, she took pleasure in handcrafting rag and corncob dolls for me. It was very special to play with such old-fashioned toys, and I treasured those dolls for over sixty years.

Then, I donated them, along with Granny's antiques, to Mountain Heritage Center Museum on the campus of Western Carolina University (my *alma mater*). Other rag dolls have been donated, but the corncob doll Granny constructed is the only one of its kind in the museum. The unique design is an ongoing testament to mountain creativity.

The simple, corncob body recalled eras when mountain ladies couldn't afford store-bought dolls for their little girls. Quite ingeniously, they learned to use common farm items and in the process developed wonderful, handcrafting skills.

84. *The corncob doll that I played with on Bear Mountain now resides in the Mountain Heritage Museum at Western Carolina University. Along with other old-fashioned toys, it is used in educational programs to preserve mountain cultural history.*

For the doll, Granny selected five corncobs of varying lengths. The longest cob served as the main body, neck, and head. The next longest became the legs, and the shortest cobs were for the arms. These were securely tied together with twine that had been unraveled and saved from the tops of 50-lb. sacks of flour.

Next, she hand-sewed a fabric head and body and stuffed them with thick wads of cotton. This padding hid most of the corncobs, so only the arms and legs showed.

To add personality to the doll, she hand-embroidered features on the cloth face: dark eyebrows, eyelashes, eyes, nose, and a smiling, red mouth.

Embroidery-thread hair showed underneath an old-fashioned bonnet that tied under the chin. Granny designed undies, a slip featuring hand-crocheted lace, and a flour-sack-print dress with ruffled sleeves. After she sewed the colorful outfit and dressed the new doll, it seemed to smile even more broadly.

Black cloth shoes with bows added a finishing touch—and I thought the completed doll was quite special and wonderful. It had taken Granny several days of measuring, cutting, sewing, stuffing, embroidering, and crocheting to create such a work of art from throw-away corncobs.

Ordinarily, the dry cobs were used to kindle the fire on cold mornings. However, in Granny's talented hands, plain corncobs were transformed into a treasured toy.

Such ingenuity shows that recycling isn't just a modern trend. Mountain folks traditionally repurposed common items (like the flour-sack twine that bound the corncobs together). After completing bigger projects from multicolored flour sacks, Granny further recycled the remaining scraps to piece quilts—and to make doll clothes.

Today, her resourceful, imaginative use of dried corncobs and free flour sacks, continues to be celebrated in educational displays at the museum. Modern people can marvel, as I still do, that Granny transformed such cast-offs into a special toy. A comical example was an occasion when a secretary returned from lunch and walked through the museum. She overheard a father explaining the display of my childhood toys to his children: "These are the kinds of toys children played with in the olden days. They didn't have electronics back then."

Since I lived with my grandparents on Bear Mountain during the 1940s, that era must have qualified as being the "olden days." Think of old-fashioned toys from your childhood, especially if they were made at home. Compare these with the complexity of modern, high-tech toys and recall the joys of simple playthings back then.

Colorful oilcloth tablecloths were popular table coverings

The name, oilcloth, comes from the late 1700s when cloth was first glazed with a mixture of boiled linseed oil to make it water resistant. Great improvements were made over time, and modern "oilcloth" is quite thin because of being manufactured with newly invented vinyl.

*85. Cousin Alice Barnwell McDonald still uses
old-fashioned oilcloth for its happy colors and practicality.*

The coated fabric available in the late 1940s and early 1950s was also known as oilcloth, though it was quite a bit thicker than modern-day versions.

Mountain ladies like Granny enjoyed oilcloth tablecloths for everyday use because the popular material was durable and colorful. Since it cost about 49 cents a yard in those days, oilcloth was also quite economical.

Multicolored fruit or flower designs were especially welcome in mountain kitchens built with plain, board walls. Farm wives could easily wipe spills with a dampened flour-sack dishcloth, and the vibrant colors didn't fade.

After several months of hard use, however, the tablecloth would begin to crack and expose the webbed, cotton backing. Then, Granny knew it was time to make one of her rare trips to the "dime store" in town.

She and I walked more than two miles down the mountain, waited for the Hendersonville city bus, and finally arrived at F. W. Woolworth's 5 and 10 Cent Store on Main Street.

On the back wall, perhaps ten choices were exhibited on pull-down rollers (window-shade style). Each oilcloth was at least four feet wide and could be purchased in lengths to fit any table.

If she had flower designs before, maybe she'd enjoy fruits this time. Granny appreciatively touched one, and then the other, as she studied the "wipeable tablecloth" display.

I could certainly see why she shopped so thoughtfully; the choices were almost mind-boggling:

Purple grape clusters on a lavender background were pictured with golden apples. Bright strawberries and cherries were scattered through the repeating pattern—across the entire width.

Red apples with a cream-colored background was another possibility. The apples were attractively arranged with decorative pears, oranges and sprinkles of blueberries and raspberries throughout the design.

Multicolored flower patterns were just as irresistible: Wide-open pink roses and creamy camellias with green leaves contrasted nicely with a dark-blue background.

Late-summer motifs featuring golden sunflowers with green leaves interspersed with cascading bunches of daisies were exhibited on what looked like a blue sky.

Although darker options, perhaps blurred winter-brown leaves in squares outlined in black, were usually available, Granny seldom chose such dull patterns.

A new oilcloth cover was supposed to lift the spirits of those at her table, and set the mood for an entire meal. It brightened the kitchen during the summer and through the long winter. Happy colors always helped when she was stringing beans or peeling potatoes.

She imagined how each dominant color might look on the table, as she made her final decision and paid the nice lady at Woolworth's.

This time the pink-rose floral pattern won, but she almost went for the grape design. She kept it in mind for later, as we hurried back to her mountain home to display the new oilcloth in time for Grandpa's supper.

Though Granny used a snowy linen cloth for company dinners, she and Grandpa always enjoyed bright-flowered oilcloth, especially at breakfast.

Think about the durable, oilcloth table coverings you remember in older relatives' kitchens years ago.

Try counting the colors you recall in each design. There will be a lot of them—and they will all be vibrant, happy, and beautiful.

Postum was an old-time coffee substitute

The price of coffee in the late 1940s and early 1950s tended to be about 37 cents a pound. Occasionally the cost would rise dramatically for a period of time. This was so upsetting that some folks felt a moral responsibility to stop buying it, even if they had the money.

It is interesting to compare our modern-day response to price increases in basic groceries. We may grimace or scowl, but we usually toss our favorite brands in the cart anyway.

Almost seventy years ago, however, my grandparents and many other mountain people totally boycotted coffee until the price came back down.

For breakfast, they temporarily switched to a powdered, roasted-grain, hot drink known as Postum. Like most every-body else, they disliked the flavor but continued buying it (for weeks or months) to demonstrate their deep frustration with current coffee prices.

I remember their long conversations with the kinfolk. Everybody lamented the sudden spike in the cost of Maxwell House coffee—their favorite brand.

Like the advertisement said, it had been "Good to the Last Drop," and now they had to drink syrupy, molasses-flavored

Postum. Teasingly, they placed "bets" on who could hold out the longest, but they all started buying coffee again, sooner or later.

86. Old-time Postum was advertised as a caffeine-free alternative to coffee.

Though Postum had been around a long time, most mountain people just never developed a taste for it. In the 1890s, Dr. J. H. Kellogg (of the corn flakes company) created a cereal-based coffee substitute that Mr. C. W. Post drank when he was a guest at the Kellogg health sanitarium.

Mr. Post liked the idea, but not the flavor. Being a sharp businessman, he thought there might be a market for a hot-drink alternative to coffee and tea.

So, back at his own headquarters, he experimented with a richer-flavored recipe. Naming it for himself, he began selling the new breakfast product as Postum Cereal Coffee.

One of the first to utilize extensive product promotion, Mr. Post began an aggressive advertising campaign urging consumers to substitute Postum for coffee and tea.

Before truth-in-advertising guidelines, the ads were worded to indicate that caffeine in coffee and tea could cause nervousness, weakness, tremors, pale eyes and skin— and even a cowardly, fearful attitude.

Hot Postum, Mr. Post insisted, was rich, fragrant, and delicious. The golden-brown, coffee substitute had to be good for you, he declared, because it was made with only four ingredients: wheat, wheat bran, molasses, and wheat flour.

The Postum Cereal Company became General Foods Corporation in 1929, and in 1988, the company merged with Kraft Foods. However, Kraft discontinued Postum in 2007 because of low sales figures.

Apparently, lots of other people agreed with Granny and Grandpa's opinion of the molasses-flavored coffee substitute.

In defense of Postum, it did become available in limited quantities again in 2013. The famous name chosen by Mr. Post was revived at the request of folks who really enjoyed the healthy breakfast alternative.

Can you recall stories of older family members who drank hot Postum, either by choice, or in protest of fluctuating coffee prices?

In the 21st century, we are more acclimated to price increases; we probably do have the "just-throw-it-in-the-cart" mentality. However, our grandparents lived in different times.

Think of kinfolks from other eras who may have been "tight as the bark on a tree" and chose to boycott common products rather than pay more—even when they had the money.

Uncle Boney's mountain cabins...and his famous names

As a child I found it intriguing that Uncle Boney was Grandpa's brother—and that he was married to Granny's sister, Aunt Rosie. That made our families doubly related, and it is easy to see how Granny and Grandpa met.

In those days, adult siblings and other kinfolks visited quite regularly. One Sunday afternoon in 1908, the entire group posed for a photograph. Uncle Boney, Aunt Rosie and their children were in front. *(See that photograph in the summer wedding story.)*

Granny and Grandpa stood on the back row, some distance apart. However, from their shy grins, it is obvious that each was aware of the other's presence. Granny must have been quite taken with Grandpa's stylish Sunday clothes. And it's almost certain he thought she was a nice-looking young lady.

Then, one day in 1909, they walked four miles to the North Carolina and South Carolina state line to meet the minister. As the outdoor ceremony began, the entire wedding party stepped across the border. That way, Granny and Grandpa were actually married in South Carolina.

The state boundary was a popular venue for local weddings in the early 1900s. North Carolina had required marriage licenses since 1870, but South Carolina didn't issue them until 1911.

Mountain folks have traditionally resisted "red tape" and bureaucracy. During my grandparents' era, young couples preferred open-air ceremonies at the state line—and kept marriage records in the family Bible.

Over the years, Granny and Grandpa bought the 1895 farmhouse on Bear Mountain that had glass windows and interior doors, one of which opened into the kitchen. However, Uncle Boney and Aunt Rosie lived in a real log cabin with a separate kitchen cabin built a safe distance downhill.

87. Uncle Boney's cabin became a bunkhouse
when his property was eventually sold to a boys' camp.

The concept of two cabins originated with the first settlers. In the event of fire, this tradition ensured that at least one structure and its furnishings could have been saved.

Flames were difficult to control in makeshift chimneys, and remote mountain homes could quickly burn to the ground. When panthers still roamed the mountains, pioneer families needed immediate access to shelter in an emergency. Hand cutting more logs required days, so having a second cabin was the best "fire insurance" available to brave colonizers.

By the late 1940s, Uncle Boney and Aunt Rosie's farm was very old and quite secluded in our Henderson County mountains. During frequent childhood visits, I was fascinated with their pioneer-style lives.

On the mile-long walk from the state road, I preferred wading the creek to avoid the treacherous foot log. Squeezing wet sand between my toes in the rippling stream was great fun in midsummer, though such amusement wasn't an option in colder weather.

Situated on a pleasant, isolated knoll, their one-room cabin had a wooden floor, two doors, but no windows. The bedroom area (in the back) stayed dark throughout the day, as well as at night. The only light came from the fireplace, kerosene lamps, or in warmer weather, through the open doors.

The separate kitchen was nice in summer, as well, though it was uncomfortable during winter. I remember the cold walk down the hill from the main cabin. Then, the log kitchen never seemed to get warm from the fires built just at mealtime.

However, Aunt Rosie's good, country cooking was on the order of Granny's with creative recipes using the available farm vegetables. Older kinfolk, who also enjoyed her company dinners, speak very fondly of Aunt Rosie's sweet spirit of hospitality. Her many talents in the kitchen haven't been forgotten—even after seventy years.

Like Granny and Grandpa, they lived a good life on their mountain farm. A story I recall was Uncle Boney's Christmas celebration. In addition to buying what he could afford for the family, he always purchased a sack of cottonseed meal for the cow's Christmas gift.

He reckoned she would enjoy a tasty, holiday treat along with dried fodder from the farm. And Uncle Boney wanted to show appreciation for the milk and butter the family cow supplied throughout the year.

The sturdy log cabin survived decades after he and Aunt Rosie both passed away in 1949. Eventually, their mountain was sold to a boys' summer camp. A substantial wooden bridge was constructed over the rushing creek, new buildings were added, and modern amenities like telephones, electricity, and running water were connected.

But Uncle Boney's original cabin was preserved and fitted with bunk beds for campers. Modern city children had the opportunity to sleep in a genuine log cabin where mountain people had lived—years before these campers were born. What a great summer experience!

When my husband and I visited the Foxfire Museum in Mountain City, GA, he was amazed at my reaction to the recreated log cabins. Though some structures had windows, I was immediately taken back in time to Uncle Boney's mountain home place.

The cabins at Foxfire seemed to be very familiar and not at all like a tourist attraction. The thick, log walls, tin roofing, open fireplaces, and heavy doors were strikingly reminiscent of my childhood visits with Uncle Boney and Aunt Rosie.

The Foxfire organization had relied on local people for guidance in reconstructing and preserving the past—with authentic realism. I so enjoyed the warm sense of kinship and happy memories the cabins evoked.

Another interesting characteristic about mountain people like Uncle Boney is how often they were named for famous individuals, i.e., Victoria, Galileo, Lincoln, Columbus, Raleigh, Edison, or Lafayette. Often, both first and middle names were included, Ulysses S., Grover Cleveland, etc.

Some of these local names were from renowned people who lived in the 1800s, though others were centuries older. Mr. Dean Ward, my elementary teacher and principal, also noticed this Appalachian phenomenon. He often wished more people could appreciate the heritage and history behind their famous names.

I wonder if Uncle Boney (1880-1949) ever knew the story of the great man from whom he was given both his first and middle names: Napoleon Bonaparte (1769-1821).

Considering the lack of public education in the mountains during the 1800s, how did Great-Grandma Jane (1842-1937) hear of the past Emperor of France? Since she probably could not read, why did she choose the full name of a historical military leader for her son—and then select the nickname, Boney?

It is fun to imagine that the lady of the Flat Rock summer estate (for whom Jane worked as a laundress beginning in 1865) told stories while Jane ironed. Southern plantation owners' wives were well educated, usually in private finishing schools, and often had traveled abroad.

Perhaps her employer was a great student of history and regaled Jane with exciting tales of the Old Countries. She could have been of French descent (maybe related to the aristocracy) and had a special interest in Napoleon's conquests.

Obviously, such fictional possibilities are probably not true.

However, Uncle Boney, who lived in a log cabin in our mountains, was somehow given the full name of one of the most famous men in French history.

Think about your ancestors who were perhaps named for historical figures. How do you imagine their names were chosen?

Even if you never enjoyed tasty meals in a separate log kitchen, recall childhood visits to older kinfolks' interesting homes. Share old photographs and stories about their lives with the younger generation—who may not have heard about their own fascinating heritage.

Riding on an old-time steam train

The extreme Saluda grade delayed rail service to Hendersonville for decades. The completed track (still the steepest in the U.S.) became an engineering marvel when the dangerous mountainside was finally conquered with picks, shovels, and convict labor.

88. Current sign in Saluda, NC, declaring the railroad to be the steepest in the U.S. When trains arrived here in 1878, another year was needed to complete rail service to Hendersonville.

Great-Grandma Jane Surrett Russell was among the 3,000 jubilant Henderson County residents who gathered to witness the arrival of the first train on July 4, 1879. Like others in that excited, anxious crowd, she had never seen (or heard) a train.

Even in the distance, the whistle was louder than folks were expecting; it seemed to shriek and moan over the mountaintops. Shaking the ground and running faster than a galloping horse, the approaching engine terrified dogs, chickens, "young'uns" and quite a few grown-ups, too.

Amid clouds of soot and smoke, it screeched to a stop at the corner of Seventh Avenue and Maple Street. In their wildest dreams, mountain people had not imagined the actual height of an "iron horse." Cinders flew, bells clanged, billows of steam spurted between the wheels—and Great Grandma Russell saw it all first hand. No wonder she talked about such a breath-taking experience for the rest of her life!

By the early 1900s, Grandpa Russell was old enough to get a coveted railroad job. The steady salary of ten cents an hour was the best pay in the country. He walked 2 1/2 miles to work, six days a week, and willingly laid the required fourteen cross ties—daily. He survived Depression-era layoffs, and his salary gradually increased. Grandpa proudly retired in 1949 just as the beloved steam trains were also being retired from their long years of service.

Southern Railway was the first major railroad to convert from steam to diesel, and mountain people mourned the change. Modern locomotives seemed to be about fuel efficiency and profits; diesels just didn't have the romance or history of the chugging, coal-driven engines.

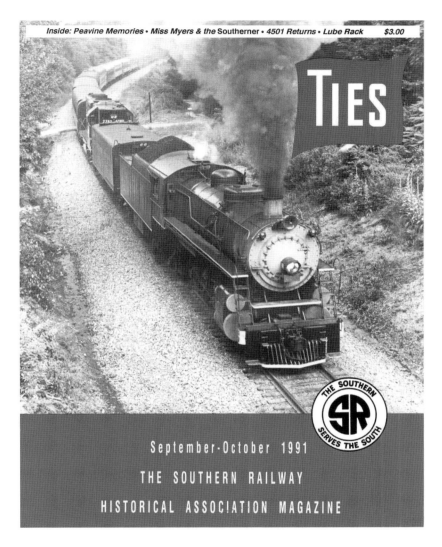

89. The cover of Janie Mae's copy of a Ties magazine depicts a steam train traveling in the mountains of Western North Carolina near the areas where Grandpa worked so many years.

Having met mail trains for years at the Post Office, Mama was as loyal to steam trains as her father and grandmother. *(See photo in old-time postal service story.)* Since the changeover to diesel was implemented gradually, she listened with dismay as fewer steam-whistle shrieks reverberated across the mountains.

She knew if her children ever had the chance to ride an old-time train, she needed to plan a short trip soon. Watching schedules carefully, she determined when a steam-powered passenger train would pass through Zirconia with stops at Tuxedo and East Flat Rock. With tickets in hand, she, little brother, and I, waited excitedly as it roared 'round the bend.

Having driven us to the station, Daddy took off in his Ford pick-up trying to beat the train to East Flat Rock (five miles away). It would be a bragging point for years if he could say his Ford was faster than a speeding train.

Though I was quite young, I remember the loud screeching and clanging, and the nice African-American conductor. Wearing a flashy uniform with big, gold buttons, he very kindly helped me up the tall, metal steps. He joined in our excitement as Mama explained our steam-train ride. Perhaps the aging conductor regretted the passing of the old engines, too. He graciously ushered us to facing window seats to watch the blurry trees as the train picked up speed.

But I was more impressed with the deep, puffy, upholstered chairs. Admiring the white linen cloths draped over the high backs, I relished the luxuriousness of the fancy train. When prompted, I hesitantly stood to see the engine—many cars ahead—puffing clouds of smoke as the train rounded a sharp mountain curve.

Too soon, we arrived at the East Flat Rock depot, and there Daddy was proudly sitting in his really fast Ford truck. We thanked the kind conductor again as he helped us down the steps, and he smilingly congratulated two little mountain children on their exciting, historic train ride.

Four generations in my family, and perhaps as many in yours, were directly impacted by the amazing steam train that climbed the Saluda grade to Hendersonville back in 1879.

Photo Credits

Figure 1: Winter snow; **Figure 3**: Roland Hoots; **Figure 8**: Christmas "pokes"; **Figure 9**: M.A. Pace Store; **Figure 10**: New Year's meal; **Figure 11**: Paper dolls; **Figure 14**: Checker players; **Figure 15**: Leon Morgan, "pokes"; **Figure 16**: Country Hawkins, lamp; **Figure 18**: Country Hawkins, quilt; **Figure 19**: Breakfast on hearth; **Figure 20**: Spring flowers on Bear Mtn.; **Figure 23**: Duster patterns, 1950s; **Figure 24**: CPO Graham Jackson; **Figure 27**: Spring lettuce and onions; **Figure 28**: Granny's flowers; **Figure 38**: Myron Steppe, garden; **Figure 39**: Annie Albertson, garden; **Figure 40**: Mullinax family garden; **Figure 42**: Turtle with tomatoes; **Figure 43**: Country Hawkins, radio; **Figure 48**: David Stallings, bee hives; **Figure 49**: Bee Masters Sourwood; **Figure 50**: James Poe, bee hives; **Figure 51**: Poe's Backyard honey; **Figure 52**: Railroad tracks with weeds; **Figure 53**: Chicken-design wall border; **Figure 54**: Echo Mtn. Inn, organ; **Figure 55**: Turkey at home place; **Figure 56**: Fall corn field; **Figure 57**: Corn in iron pot; **Figure 58**: Corn and corn muffins; **Figure 60**: Splitting wood on Bear Mtn.; **Figure 61**: Mandy Gibson; woodstove;

Figure 62: Country Hawkins; biscuits; **Figure 63**: Country Hawkins, cabinet; **Figure 64**: Larry, Janie Mae, wood stove; **Figure 65**: Ardie Gallant, pie; **Figure 66**: Henderson's sweet potatoes; **Figure 67**: Eight-layer pumpkin pie; **Figure 71**: Flour sacks on Bear mtn.; **Figure 76**: Granny's spring; **Figure 77**: Leon Morgan, buckets; **Figure 82**: Royal Blue Band, harmonica; **Figure 85**: Alice McDonald's oilcloth; **Figure 86**: Postum container; **Figure 88**: Saluda Grade sign; Photos by Larry McKinley

Figure 2: Granny's parents; **Figure 4**: Dean A. Ward; **Figure 12**: Maybin's Grocery; **Figure 22**: Janie Mae's Easter suit; **Figure 26**: Sgt. York, WWI hero; **Figure 29**: Bess and Virgie Russell; **Figure 30**: Granny and Janie Mae; **Figure 33**: Montraville Lafayette Jones; **Figure 34**: Antique car, teenagers; **Figure 35**: Antique car, young man; **Figure 36**: Antique car, children; **Figure 37**: Granny; **Figure 44**: Granny, Grandpa, 1908; **Figure 45**: Janie Mae's parents, 1942; **Figure 46**: James Evance Jones, age 3; **Figure 47**: Great-Grandma Alice Pace; **Figure 59**: Virgie Russell, mail train; **Figure 69**: Dean A. Ward; **Figure 70**: Granny wearing apron; **Figure 72**: Boney, Grandpa, overalls; **Figure 73**: Catalog pictures, overalls; **Figure 78**: 1922 Sears catalog; **Figure 80**: WWII catalog page; **Figure 81**: 1912 catalog page; **Figure 89**: Steam train; Jones family photos, digitized by Larry McKinley

Figure 5: Barbara Ann; **Figure 68**: Antique mantle clock; **Figure 74**: 1865 iron wash pot; **Figure 75**: Granny's sadiron; **Figure 84**: Corncob doll in museum; **Cover photo**; Photos courtesy of

Mountain Heritage Center Museum, Western Carolina University

Figure 6: Nativity scene; Henderson family photo, used by permission

Figure 7: Wise man; **Figure 13**: Mural by Bruce Zior; **Figure 17**: Yo-yo bedspread; **Figure 21**: Creasy greens, **Figure 32**: I-26 connecting highway; **Figure 79**: Antique shoe iron; **Figure 83**: J. Blackwell, harmonica; **Figure 87**: Uncle Boney's cabin; Photos by Janie McKinley

Figure 25: Little White House; Photo by Ruth Ann McKinley Garber; used by permission

Figure 31: Fruit stand with bedspreads by Ardie Gallant, Artist. Used by permission.

Figure 41: Ellen McKinley Hughes, garden; Hughes family photo, used by permission

Index